Poker Passion

Poker Passion

✦

Place, Person, and Personality in a California Casino

Joseph Fischer

iUniverse, Inc.
New York Lincoln Shanghai

Poker Passion
Place, Person, and Personality in a California Casino

iUniverse books may be ordered through booksellers or by contacting:

iUniverse
2021 Pine Lake Road, Suite 100
Lincoln, NE 68512
www.iuniverse.com
1-800-Authors (1-800-288-4677)

ISBN-13: 978-0-595-39123-3 (pbk)
ISBN-13: 978-0-595-83509-6 (ebk)
ISBN-10: 0-595-39123-0 (pbk)
ISBN-10: 0-595-83509-0 (ebk)

Printed in the United States of America

Dedicated to all those amateur poker players who are not addicted to gambling and to their tolerant families, especially mine.

Contents

Acknowledgments

This book could only have been written with the input and cooperation of dealers, players, management and staff of the Oaks Club Casino. Almost everyone has been extremely helpful, ever ready to express their opinions and at the same time show no reluctance to challenge mine. I trust I have not offended or misrepresented any of them. I offer the usual disclaimer that "the views expressed here are mainly my own." I may have unknowingly left out some persons' names but given the size and complexity of the casino milieu and my own aging memory, I asked to be excused.

I wish in particular to thank the owner of the Oaks Club, John Tibbetts and his main managers Larry, Mike, Martin, Allen, and Stephen. There are in addition many casino staff who have been friendly and helpful including among others Wayne, Bruno, Mike, John, Bobbie, Eddy, Cole, Kingfish, Bill, Janice, Tai, Rachael, and Carol. They saw to it that I didn't lose my way to a table, kept me in a supply of chips and answered my many questions. It also has been nice to play with props who have been forthcoming including Gayle, Art, Steve, and Jay.

With respect to those ever so important employees, the dealers, I want to thank among others Su Chinn, Linda, Prum San, Louie, Robert, Steven, Bob, Kevin, Tracy, Mark, Eric, Jerry, Phillip, Bond, April, Nancy, Richard, Ruth, Bobby J., Freddie, Kevin, Bobby I., Money, Gabriel, Chea Bou, Ricardo, Howard, Michael, Virginia, Perry, and Tom—all of whom I should have tipped more but nonetheless always made sure I got two cards. I want to thank several waitresses who have served me well for many years, including Beverly, Betty, Sheila, Huong, Leann, and Casey. I would be remiss in not recognizing certain players who have sat at a poker table with me and who have given me both enjoyment and trouble. Among these are Ron, Paul, Minnie, Frank, Charlie, Taipple R., Diego, Dennis, Peter, John, Henry, Jeff, Robb, Toby, Gee Gee, Boomer, Nas, Bob, Jack, Bob H., Mark, Carmen, Red, Bill, Chris, Monday, Danny, Don, Malcolm, Skip, Yang, Vincent, Kim, Drake, Dieter, Oscar, Remo, Ray, Omar, Doc, Moe, Ray, Caroll, Jim, Rick, JoJo, Adam, Sam, Paul, Dick, Harry, John, Patrick, Fred, Reza and too many others to mention. And finally there are my long-standing backyard poker pals, past and present: Vance, Jerry, Roger, Ed, Chicken, Tom, Bob, Bud, David, Carol, Gary, and Dan. They have tolerated my quirks for many decades. I would thank them much more but they all owe me money! And to Clare, my constant companion, supporter and helpmate, and to my computer wiz David.

Preface

In the United States poker is fast becoming the all-American game. Casinos and card rooms are everywhere—on moored barges, on Native American reservations, and in grandiose hotels, spread out in a variety of cities and states throughout the nation. The keen interest in poker is a reflection of the ever-exploding popularity of gambling. However, poker now probably attracts more gamblers than car, horse, and dog races combined. Both amateurs and professionals, a growing number of women and high school and college students are all involved in this game of chance, lured by large and small financial rewards and the excitement of competition. All know that there are more losers than winners, but this seems not to be a deterrence to willing participants.

This book has very little to do with success or failure at poker. It focuses on a single large casino and one particular game (Texas Hold'em). It is the result of participation, observations, and interviews by the author for over twenty-five years. It draws lightly upon anthropology, sociology, and psychology. It is the author's way of retrieving in book form a lifetime of experience in playing poker. Although most of the information comes from my experience in one casino, it is meant to have a wider meaning and application to casino gambling and poker-playing in general throughout the United States.

I. Prologue: Personal Stuff and Poker Journeys

I vaguely remember my first experience with poker occurred when I was four or five years old while visiting my grandparents in New York City. My grandfather taught me to play a simplified version of five-card stud. We used my grandmother's collection of buttons as chips. I have actually seen a photograph of me seated at their dining room table with a deck of cards in my hand and these buttons in front of me. The photograph has long since disappeared but I remember being given one of my grandfather's half-done pickles as a reward for playing with him. To this day the only pickles I will eat are those green ones. Poker and pickles! Talk about imprinting! I cannot recall whether I won many of those buttons. I was most attracted to the picture cards (kings, queens, and jacks) which reminded me of the small lead toy soldiers that I often played with. If I remember correctly I thought in order to win a hand you had to have at least two of these cards, which as it turned out much later in my life was not too far from the truth.

When I was about ten years old my parents and I lived in the Brighton Beach Hotel in Brooklyn. It was an aging building covered by half dead vines; the so-called garden in front usually had a fine crop of dandelion weeds. The hotel was an inexpensive home to jobless persons and particularly unemployed actors. I recall four members of a European trapeze family and an ex-Shakespearean actor who went about citing profundities to anyone who would listen from Hamlet, Othello, or whatever came into his mind. In the room next door to us was a couple who had a noisy parrot that supposedly had a twenty-word vocabulary.

I only recall him saying over and over again, "Don't do it, don't do it." His chattering often kept myself and my parents awake at night. Once my father who was a pharmacist suggested that the bird might benefit from a sleeping pill.

In the hotel basement there was a poker game going on day and night. It was only suspended for the Jewish High Holy days. Both of my parents played alternately hoping to help pay the room rent. The stakes were from one to three dollars which in 1936 was a considerable amount. When I got home from school I would go down to the basement and ask one of my parents for a poker chip which was worth fifty cents. I took the chip and cashed it in; I immediately went outside to buy three chocolate doughnuts. These were available in the late afternoon from a Dugan's Bakery truck which sounded a loud bell as it slowly passed our hotel. I took my doughnuts to my room and enjoyed them with a pint of Borden's milk. Giving me a chip meant to me, mistakenly, that my parents were always winning at poker. I never remembered being denied a chip unless I brought home a report card with bad grades. Fortunately I was a super student and to this day I remember with nostalgia and fondness those days and those poker games when I was ten. Cards, chips, doughnuts, Shakespeare, and bird squawks have forever framed that time for me.

My first experience with poker as an adult occurred in 1943 when I was an undergraduate at a small Pennsylvania college. I expected to join the Navy in a few months so I was not much interested in studying. A group of about six students shared an old house and meals. On weekends we often drove to nearby Wheeling, West Virginia, which reputedly had the largest steel mills and the biggest red-light district in the United States. Of course, it was the latter which interested us. During the three winter months of my stay at this college it seemed to snow heavily all the time which provided us with ample opportunities to launch snowballs from a second-story window at passing cars. We played small stakes poker irregularly on rainy nights and no one seemed concerned about studies or classes. World War II was on and all of us were just biding time. My memories are hazy but I remember that five of us played poker most often. One of our group was quite hard of hearing but we made every effort to see to it that he understood what was being said. The chap in the poker game that I remember most vividly was an amateur magician who often did card tricks for us. He could deal you a good hand and deal himself a better one by manipulating the cards. However, I don't recall him ever doing this when we played for money. We were all at different times winners and losers; it was a friendly game. However, my experience with our card magician taught me at least five things: be alert while playing, take nothing for granted, know that there are players who are much better than you, eat a hearty meal before playing in case you go broke, and always save money for carfare. In the years since I probably violated those dictums more than once such is the nature of poker players.

I cannot recall thinking about poker again until I was a sailor during World War II from 1944-1946. I was a young helmsman on the U.S.S. Oklahoma City (CL-91), a light cruiser designed to repel enemy planes. It has long since died somewhere in a junkyard. Ship rules forbade gambling games but many took place on the sly including dice and poker. Draw poker was the favorite game aboard ship. We organized games at night with six to eight off-duty players. We used the floor of our sleeping compartment for a table with a blanket as a cover. One of the sailors was paid to be a lookout if officers approached; however, they rarely bothered us. Bets were from one to ten dollars, always in cash not chips. We used the same three decks of cards over and over again until they almost fell apart. They were too precious to throw away. All the cards appeared to be marked with scratches, food stains, and cigarette burns.

On one memorable occasion we were playing poker in one of the upper deck navigation rooms near the ship's bridge. It was a room used for radar to track planes and other ships. All this was done on a glossy glass oval table full of numbers and diagrams. This was our poker table for the evening. We used chips rather than cash and on this one occasion there were about ten players each with various amounts of chips stacked in front of them. Without warning the senior duty officer entered the radar room. We knew him as a stern disciplinarian and a fine sailor whom we all respected but did not like. We called him "Dapper Dan" because he was always impressively dressed. He looked coldly and calmly at the table full of chips and with his white-gloved hands mixed them all up. We all afterwards expected the worst: to be put on "report," get fined or other punishments. However, he made no comment and left the room as abruptly as he had entered it. And so there we were sailors acting as poker players, under full steam in the mid-Pacific ocean, in the middle of a war, facing a huge pile of mixed chips. The irony did not escape me at the time. Now we had to decide which chips belonged to which player. It took us about an hour after some dickering to arrive at an equitable distribution. We never again used the radar room for poker. We later learned that the officer never reported the incident. The war was about to end and my naval poker career was over.

After being discharged in 1946 I returned to my small hometown in western New York State. Immediately upon my return I learned that almost every Saturday night there was a poker game in the basement of the local synagogue. It was a place I was very familiar with, having been Bar Mitzvahed there in 1940. The synagogue basement was used for social gatherings, fundraising, Bible study, Hebrew lessons, and canasta. So playing poker there was not inappropriate. In any case the resident rabbi either took no notice or merely looked the other way. There were food and drinks but mainly it was an informal group of young and old amateur players, all of whom were friends and part of a small Jewish community. We only played draw poker and you could win or lose no more than fifty dollars. For all I know it may have been the only ongoing gambling game in a synagogue in the United States. It was in this "religious" setting that I truly cut my teeth on learning the game of poker.

My first experience with casino poker was in Las Vegas en route by car to California in 1950. I stayed on what was called "the strip" in an inexpensive but pleasant hotel/casino called the Hacienda. It was modeled after a Mexican dwelling with a terra cotta roof and stucco walls decorated with colorful tiles. The garden was mostly cactus. I did not play much at this casino because there only enough games in the evening and even these were meager. The Hacienda may have been the second oldest casino in Las Vegas; it no longer exists. I remember someone trying to sell me a sombrero.

On the first day I played seven-card stud in the Sands Casino and in a few hours because of luck rather than skill I won about one hundred dollars. Free drinks were available to any player and there was a sumptuous buffet of Mexican food that cost two dollars. This, however, did not compensate me for losing all my money the next day. I was determined somehow to recoup my losses lest I be stranded in this desert city. My unwise solution was to risk cashing a bad check. I went up to the cashier's cage and was given money without any confirmation of my credit or bank account. I returned to the poker game, made up for all my losses and redeemed my bad check. I remember asking the cashier whether this was a common occurrence. She said with a laugh, "Are you kidding!" In today's casinos such a thing would never be permitted. You would be trusted only as far as your money in the bank. The experience taught me a lesson and ever since I have always left my checkbook behind when playing casino poker and never have used credit cards to obtain cash. I have usually resisted the temptation to gamble beyond my means. Every once in a while I forget the admonition and all you poker players out there know what I mean.

The number of home or private poker games in the United States has never been accurately calculated but it must be in the thousands or, more probably, in the millions. During my tenure at the University of California in Berkeley I was involved in a home game with a group of fellow academicians. There was an educator (myself), three anthropologists, a political scientist, a book seller and a poet. It was a modest small stakes game played about once a month. It was not very serious poker; it was hard to win or lose more than thirty dollars. All of us knew each other, were congenial and always seemed to enjoy the game. I have pleasant memories of this time which abruptly ended with demonstrations against the war in Vietnam. I looked elsewhere to pursue poker and found that the same Hacienda Casino that I had stayed at before provided free air roundtrips between San Francisco and Las Vegas. When we arrived at the hotel we were given ten dollars worth of chips and a chit for a free meal. It was a great deal but it didn't last long. The Federal Aviation Administration grounded the plane labeling it unsafe. Never mind that the plane in question was a DC-6 and that this type had been flown almost without incident during the four years of World War II under conditions of monsoons, typhoons, and snowstorms. I am sure political pressure from regular commercial airlines were responsible for the short life of Hacienda Air. It had been a boon for a bachelor and gambler like me. No doubt there will never be the likes of it again. So much for progress!

Another of my home poker experiences involved a risky no-limit game in which you could easily win or lose a thousand dollars. The game usually lasted until two or three in the morning. When my bachelor days ended so did my participation in this game upon a strong ultimatum from my wife to do so or else. In any case the risks were too high, the time spent too long, and the anxieties too intense.

For the last thirty years I have been part of what I call a "backyard" poker group. It is remarkable in that its members have hardly changed and ten of us continue to play in a backyard cottage every Wednesday evening. We have lost some players due to divorce, changing jobs, and in one case to suicide. We play modestly high stakes; you can win or lose usually no more than one hundred dollars. We play a bewildering number of poker games, many of which we have invented, most of which are not conventional and never played in a casino. At one time I counted some thirty-five different games that we played. These included Omaha, Lincoln, Nebraska, Sudden Death, Traffic Speaks

Disaster, Trombone, Bunches, John Wayne, Shopping Cart, Jacks or Back, Value Jet, Two by Two, Pass the Trash, Six and Seven Card Stud and many other variations with features too numerous to mention or describe. Needless to say this array of poker games are intimidating unless you have played with them as long as we have. Newcomers are welcome but understandably we have not been able to recruit many. One game we seldom play is Texas Hold'em, the most popular poker game in the U.S. We regard it as too tame, too conventional, and a welcome change from this poker game that is the one most played in all casinos.

Our longevity for over thirty years as a poker group is extraordinary in U.S. society for a group of men to stick together that long for any reason. We have played together, we have gambled in Lake Tahoe and Las Vegas together, we have shared meals in fancy restaurants, we have gone to art exhibitions, shared weddings and a funeral, have gone to baseball games, and have exchanged our card-playing experiences with each other. Our poker game binds and bonds us in a fashion, has created a pleasant environment, increased our sociability, and at this juncture seems our game will go on forever. As I age and overcome various illnesses it is nice to look forward to every Wednesday evening. I do not share in the pizza or beer that is offered. I rely on tea and Oreo cookies. And added to all this are my happy visits to a local casino. Ah, the good life!

II. Call This an Introduction

This book is absolutely not about how to play or win at poker. There are already some one hundred and thirty-three books in print that do this. Clearly another similar book on poker seems hardly needed. There are, however, almost no books that describe what goes on among and around poker players inside a card club or casino. This is strange because gambling with cards in casinos has become one of the largest expanding pursuits and enterprises in the United States. This book deals with ordinary players in one modest-sized casino. There is nary an anecdote about famous professional gamblers and big-time tournament winners. Furthermore, this book only contains what I have personally experienced, solicited, or observed. It rises or falls on my ears, eyes, and brain to make sense of what is going on. The validity of my descriptions and understandings are open to all to criticize or affirm. In northern California where I live casinos are everywhere and new ones are being built. There is a veritable explosion of gambling casinos not only here but across the United States. The poker game, its patrons, and the environment in which it takes place are at the center of this phenomenon. It is this combination that I will examine in this book.

Presented here then is an inside and first-hand look at a particular game of poker (Texas Hold'em), its players, and one casino that I have played in for over twenty years. It is the Oaks Club in Emeryville, California, situated between the cities of Oakland and Berkeley, just a ten-minute drive from where I live. My focus has little to say about the strategies of poker or casinos in general. I make no claims that playing poker may be a rewarding, satisfying, or a sensible activity for others.

Poker players may desire to get rich quick, to pursue an exciting challenge, to fill up empty time, or to enjoy the recreation. I myself qualify for membership in all these four motivations. For me the benefits and disappointments have over time sort of equalized themselves with slightly more gains than losses. Of course, my time playing poker in a casino perhaps could have been better directed to constructive things elsewhere. Writing this book serves as a kind of justification and expiation for playing poker so often and over such a long time. In a sense I am retrieving my experiences beyond the boundaries of defeats and victories.

This book is not intended as an advertisement for the Oaks Club or an evaluation of how it conducts its business. It is also not intended as a promotion of gambling or, for that matter, the playing of poker, however much I seem to extol its virtues. Rather its sole focus is on the institution itself and its patrons. I have further limited my observations in the casino to only one poker game, Texas Hold'em, and its two limit games, 3/6 and 6/12. It is this game in which I have been a participant; the experience then is firsthand. This focus meets some of the major social science requirements for conducting an inquiry. These come primarily from anthropology, sociology and, to a lesser extent, from psychology. A primary requirement for reliable description and analysis are narrow, well-defined parameters. This one casino, its limited scale and modest size compared to large Nevada casinos enable this kind of focus. I thus regard myself smugly as an "expert participant observer" who relies on both subjective and objective resources. I have interviewed some players and casino employees to round out and test my observations. Hopefully they will critique what I have written.

The gambling casino, its patrons, its games, and its environment represent a kind of microcosm of human behavior in a distinct social setting. In this case it is poker which connects the four categories and although they do not necessarily imitate life they come close to doing so. Because of this my passion for the game of poker is motivated by many more things than playing, winning, or losing. In the Oaks Club I find myself in the midst of an engaging cultural and social milieu that I love to describe. And that is mostly what this book is about. Join me as I traverse this particular gambling path. You don't need cards or chips for the tour. I am reminded by a famous aficionado of the game that "poker is not a life or death game; it is more important than that."

III. A Bit of History

In 1773 in his book, *Tour to the Hebrides*, the renowned English writer and lexicographer, Samuel Johnson, had this to say about cards. "I am sorry I have not learned to play at cards. It is very useful in life: it generates kindness and consolidates society." Of course, he says nothing about gambling and it is certainly far from the realities of card games like poker in today's world. Most dictionaries and card books state the origins of poker are at best obscure. The word may be a modification of the French term *paque* which is a card game similar to poker. It may also have been derived from the combined German words *poch* and *spiel* which means a "bragging" game. Poker is generally defined as a "card-game for two or more persons, each of which bets on the value of his hand and may win by holding the highest hand on an established system of rank or by bluffing others into ceasing to compete." In simpler terms it is a money wagering game played with cards, mostly by men in homes, small card rooms, and large casinos. Today you can also add the Internet to this list.

Poker was first mentioned in print in the United States about 1836 but the game certainly existed before in New Orleans after the Louisiana Purchase in 1803. The cradles of poker were the gambling saloons and Mississippi steamboats. It was often described then as a game peopled by con-men, crooks, cheats, wealthy dilettantes, and professional gamblers. This characterization has long since given way to defining gambling in general and poker in particular as a recreation and an entertainment.

Poker is played mostly by adult men of all ages and from a variety of social class and ethnic backgrounds. It has been estimated that some

20,000,000 Americans play poker at least once a month. Its various forms found in the Oaks Club are stud, Lowball, Omaha, and Texas Hold'em, the latter now being the most popular. It has been said that poker is "not so much a card game as a game that happens to be played with cards…, the true instruments of which are the coin of the realm." Poker is perhaps "one of the most skill-demanding of all card games and is inevitably played for money because it is necessarily played with money," which is symbolized by chips. Amateur and professional players may regard themselves as experts at winning and some undoubtedly are, "but the only people who make a constant living from casino poker are casino owners." What marks all poker players is the belief that they can win. This is not as far-fetched as it sounds compared to lotto, slot machines, roulette, or dice where the odds against winning are much greater. Poker is the most highly evolved of the so-called "vying" family of games. The essence of poker relies on individual skill, experience, luck, and chance. It is a major attraction for players because it emphasizes their individual acumen and stamina if they are to succeed. And of course, most do not. In any case they as players are automatically admitted to membership in the premier game that is casino poker. It provides them an uncommon opportunity for success, seemingly at little risk and in congenial surroundings. If they are immune to addictive gambling they can fully enjoy their participation and the competition. In addition there is a kind of *macho* quality that may motivate male players. Something akin to demonstrating virility may lurk in a player's psyche. For some men poker is a kind of war game exercise or combat test that provides challenges and ego fulfillment that is not easily found in their daily life. Winners get caught up at times in an accelerating rhythm in the game. You can see it in their body language, in their quick response and provocative play. It is more than gambling; it is a particular "high" quite unlike anything else. Poker can also be looked at as a magnetic game that features many of the elements of life such as daring, patience, deception, confidence, escape, and contentment. Further it is a "hands-on" game in which each poker play can possibly control his or her fate. Too much optimism or anticipation, however, frequently will not work out.

The same poker rules apply to all players though there are minor differences from casino to casino. They can use or share the same pack of fifty-two cards and their relative ranking or fixed value is known to all players. They sit around a common table in numbered seats with a fixed number of competitors, where bets are limited and where a single dealer controls the game. Poker offers a relief from boredom and something engaging outside of work, family, and home. The game of poker is played in private homes, modest card rooms, in big casinos, and online. Many may travel considerable distances to play or watch poker where very large amounts of money may change hands. I found, however, from interviewing players that most of them come to a particular casino because of convenience. And this is true for the Oaks Club and its accessible location.

Now by way of what I hope is an entertaining digression I would like to compare casinos with another "social" institution. An attractive comparison is that between casinos and religious institutions, primarily churches and synagogues. Here I am assigning terms to each that will highlight common features. Poker could be considered for some as a "religion." The Bible is the book of casino rules. Chips and cards are its sacramental objects. Chairs are its pews and tables its altars. It's patrons could be considered parishioners, dealers are deacons and managers are ministers. Casinos like churches never close and all are welcome to enter, be they sinners or the faithful. They both attract substantial crowds on religious holidays. Food and drink are both part of communion. Table talk could be viewed as sermons. Tipping is the equivalent of Sunday morning donations. The casino fee taken out of each pot is akin to the tithe. Winning may be a kind of just salvation, losing like a penance or punishment. And there is a good deal of begging and praying done by players though for purposes other than reverence or seeking God's intervention.

I will go no further with such comparisons. I offer them up with some imagination and a little exaggeration to show the connections between what seems two very unlike institutions. There is a playful quality about doing so. I leave it up to the reader to extract some useful meaning in all this. In any case, please humor me!

IV. One Casino, One History

The Oakes Club in Emeryville, California has a long history of over one hundred years. It originated in its present location about 1896 when it was just a hotel, a bar, and a barber shop. In those days such an establishment was called a saloon and the best persons in society were not its patrons. It was not quite the dark place depicted by Hollywood movies but it was still considered beyond respectability. Gambling began in the hotel sometime before 1935 with the present owner's grandfather who had become a partner. Grandfather Tibbetts bought out his only partner about 1940. The name of the casino was changed from Congers to its present name due to the presence of the Oakland Oaks Pacific Coast baseball team that played in a field just across the street.

Grandfather was a card player who neither smoked or drank, a rarity for a gambler. He was not actively involved in the gambling side of the club. After the end of World War II, the present owner's father, Jack Tibbetts, became the owner. He ran the restaurant, closed the barber shop about 1995, kept the bar, and hired a manager to supervise all the gambling. The only card games played were lowball and five-card draw. State of California gambling rules mandated that the only legal poker games were those that did not involve common or face-up cards. On the non-permitted list were such games as stud, chemin de faire, Hokie Pokie, and several others. No women were allowed in the card rooms until 1966, one year after the Equal Rights law was passed.

In 1978 the casino could be open only twenty-four hours on week-ends; otherwise it had to close at 2:00 A.M. The site in Emeryville turned out to have been an excellent location for the Oaks Club.

Nearby were several large industries such as Pepsi Cola Bottling, the Del Monte Cannery, Judson Steel, American Tire and Rubber, and the American Can Company. All of these plants have gone but in their heyday they were a major source of patrons for the Oaks Club.

Until 1974 there were fourteen card tables allowed in the casino for lowball and pan. After a two-year struggle the casino received permission in 1984 from the City of Emeryville to start pai gow, a Chinese game played with domino-like tiles. It took three more years for the Oaks Club to get authorization to play Texas Hold'em because it required face-up cards. In 1989 the Oaks Club was greatly enlarged from the modest card room that it had been to a spacious casino. Its central gambling room covers about 10,000 square feet, with an eighteen to twenty foot high ceiling and has nineteen poker tables. In addition, there are other tables used for pai gow, double-hand poker, pan and blackjack.

Beginning in the late 1980s, the casino initiated tournaments which grew to one hundred and twelve or so over the course of a year. There is even a tournament in May only for casino employees. Tournaments became a highly visible and a lucrative part of casino business throughout California and the rest of the country. At the Oaks Club Texas Hold'em tournaments have become the number one game played and attracts many of this game's devotees. In addition, interest in Texas Hold'em has greatly accelerated due to its exposure on television and the so-called various World Series of Poker.

January 2005 marked a dramatic change in the operation of the Oaks Club. It was centered on the adoption of a new so-called "drop system." Previously all players at a given table had to pay "time," a fee the casino collected every half hour. It was four dollars for the 3/6 game and five dollars for the 6/12 game. This meant that if you left the table temporarily and your seat was still being held you were not only losing the opportunity to play one or more hands before time expired, but you were also paying for it. That is why you used to hear players complain with such statements as "You're holding up the game" or

"Deal more quickly." The new system abolished time payments except in the highest limit games (15/30, 30/60, etc.) and substituted instead a set amount collected from each winning pot. It is four dollars for both the 3/6 and 6/12 games, of which one dollar goes into a jackpot pool and three dollars for the casino. Players now are not concerned about time and in addition it is cheaper for them because the fee comes out of only winning hands. The dealer "drops" the four dollars into a sliding box that is attached to the table, the contents of which are collected at set times. This new method was more complicated than before because previously each dealer brought to the table his or her own rack of chips for which they were individually responsible and accountable. Now each table already contains a rack in place with a pre-established amount of chips. When there is a change of dealers each of them has to agree that the rack is "right." Five dollar or less shortages are absorbed by the casino and any overages are used to offset the shortage. Dealers had to quickly learn a different set of procedures. In a short time the transition though difficult in the beginning is now working well. This change was in part due to the fact that most casinos in California were already using a "no time" system and was greatly preferred by players because it was less costly. Competition among casinos to draw in and hold patrons is extremely keen. It was a significant change for an old well-established casino like the Oaks Club.

The continuing success of the Oaks Club comes in part from its prime location not far from jobs and near easy freeway access. It also resulted through amicable relations with the City of Emeryville officials. Through the years its connection with the city and what it would allow or mandate had been sometimes very trying. The Oaks Club is subject to city regulations about the games they offer, the employees they hire, the fire regulations they must follow, the sanitation requirements for the bar and the restaurant, and parking constraints. More importantly, the club is responsible to the city, county, state, and federal agencies for its taxes. It is indeed a complex enterprise to organize and run properly.

The most important factor in the Oaks Club success is due to its single family ownership over a long period which has resulted in effective administration. This has occurred in part from the Oaks Club being able to retain for a long period the loyalty and skills of its several managers. This is extremely uncommon in the business world where there is a high turnover in both management and workers. The importance of this one family ownership cannot be overstated. It has provided for itself continuity and a high profile that has survived and prospered while other local competitors have vanished.

High up on the casino walls and just below a television set are words in red moving across a screen. It shows what may be the Oaks Club motto, "Continuing 100 years of tradition and integrity." Other words on the screen admonishes patrons to "Play It Smart." I would not dispute the motto and would commend the second statement.

(Note: I have referred throughout this book to the Oaks Club as a casino. Strictly speaking it is a card club. Casinos usually have dice, roulette, slot machines, card games, and entertainment. The Oaks Club only has card games and pai gow. Casino, however, conjures up a large establishment which indeed the Oaks Club is. Card rooms are smaller and in the past connoted sleazy places in which to play. Since there are no legal requirements with respect to naming, a gambling establishment, large or small, may call itself whatever it wants.)

V. Casino Environment

What is often overlooked or taken for granted about a casino is its general atmosphere, physical setting, and décor. It is assumed that if it is a clean well-lighted place with proper circulation, good seats and decent food, nothing much more is required. However, many features of this environment affect both the reputation of the casino and the needs of its patrons. As has been stated, the main room of the Oaks Club occupies about 10,000 square feet and is not allowed to contain more than 590 persons at one time. The room is shaped like a hexagon with wooden railings on two of its sides behind which people can wait, observe or merely hang out. There are nineteen poker tables, each nine feet long around which are ten chairs for players and one for a dealer who sits in the middle. To his left seats are numbered one through ten. Small movable tables for food and drinks are alongside many of the seated players.

Cushions are available for comfort but many of them have seen better days. I myself use three of them for elevation since the height of the tables for me seem to be too low. The central room contains eight television sets for those players who wish to watch sporting events while playing. High overhead on the walls are eight installations with two cameras each that may monitor high stakes games and record any action at some of the poker tables. These may provide both security and the surveillance of rule infractions, disputes, player's behavior, and the performance of dealers. There are two chip stations in which an employee sells chips to players and reports empty seats. At one end of the central room is a kind of command center which assigns seats to players, reserves seats for players, and in general keeps track of what

19

games are going on or need to be started. There is a loudspeaker system from this vantage that pages patrons and that announces a variety of messages. When all the poker tables are full there is a constant low level din interrupted by victory cries, heated arguments, yells of anguish, and calls for service. The loudest noise occurs when a jackpot is won at a table and all the benefactors arise as a group applauding and yelling. A vexing problem that is irritating to both players and dealers is the lack of a silent communication system between the dealers and managers. It is common to hear dealers and players yelling out loud that a seat is available, that a floor manager is wanted, or that chips are needed. This is a major and ironic flaw in a million-dollar well-appointed otherwise reasonably run casino.

Almost all the poker action takes place in the large central room. When it is very crowded two smaller side rooms may be used. It is particularly crowded at night, on weekends, and holidays. A successful casino must provide a comfortable and healthy environment that makes players feel secure and does not interfere with their poker playing. However, no card room has yet been designed that completely satisfies all its patrons or employees. Complaints are common about what's on television, room temperature, air circulation, the limited space between tables, and so on. Ordinarily, floor managers take care of such things but some require nagging before doing so. There will always be cranky and whiny players that can never be satisfied. In any case the casino probably cannot be perfectly functional as well as aesthetic. In many casinos it runs the gamut from the starkness of a warehouse to that of a glitzy temple. The Oaks Club falls somewhere in the middle of these two types.

Every casino has decorations to make its rooms more attractive. However, this is a low priority and the Oaks Club is no exception. On its side walls there are five framed paintings: two with Chinese subjects, one an old painting of the casino, and two that are nondescript nature scenes. A black satin Oaks Club jacket that one can buy is displayed on a wall. Behind the railings there are eleven framed notices, one potted palm, a bookcase and a large bronze abstract sculpture. In back of the Pai Gow tables there is a very large standing lacquered Chinese screen affixed with jade flower decorations. There is one cloakroom, two restrooms, a cashier's cage, and a little room where dealers check in. There are house phones, a water cooler, a stand for free coffee and tea, and two side rooms used by waitresses. Two large electric clocks are at either end of the main room which are remnants of the abolished "time" system. Everyone can easily see the time which is in contrast to many casinos in which clocks are purposely hidden. I suppose this is done to make players unaware of time or, for that matter, whether it is day or night. The noticeable lack of windows also contributes to this. Anything to keep players playing!

The casino has a restaurant, a bar, a shoeshine stand, an ATM machine, two candy dispensers, and booths for outside phone calls. The Oaks Club as do many casinos provides a free shuttle service for local patrons as well as four parking lots to accommodate cars. All the conveniences and amenities contribute to making patrons feel comfortable and easier for them to stay and play for long hours. The casino is not exactly a home away from home but for many players it appears to be so. Many of the regular players, dealers and staff know each other on a first-name basis which contributes to a friendly atmosphere. Remember there is no entrance or membership fee, and no recreation or entertainment within casino confines except gambling. If you are thirsty there is a bar and if you are hungry there is a restaurant and table service. Casinos are the only major businesses that do not sell a product; they mostly provide a "free" opportunity for players to spend money. A pleasant well-controlled and congenial environment are essential to a profitable casino business. The physical variables and their impact, however, have yet to be studied.

The elimination of smoking was a significant turning point in the development of clean and healthy casinos. But it took more than eight decades for this to come about. Casinos like other institutions in the

U.S. society have finally come around to the view that an attractive and healthy environment is a win/win policy.

VI. Casino Management

The Oaks Club, call it a casino or a card room, is by any definition a large-scale business operation. It has over four hundred employees and perhaps attracts some 170,000 patrons a year. It welcomes gamblers, visitors, and bystanders. Some come to play regularly, some infrequently, some only to observe, some to eat or drink and some just to hang out. Persons under the age of twenty-one are prohibited by law from entering the gaming areas and adults with tank tops or bare feet are denied admission. The casino bar is open until 2:00 A.M. and the Hofbrau-type restaurant which also serves Chinese food opens at 11:00 A.M. and closes at 1:00 A.M. Food can be ordered from the kitchen at any time. Both the bar and restaurant are leased out and managed separately. The Oaks Club is mid-sized compared to Las Vegas casinos and unlike them cannot have slot machines, dice games, roulette, or sports betting on its premises. In addition, no entertainment is provided which is so big a part of Las Vegas style casinos. Casinos in California owned by Native American tribes are not subject to these limitations. Casinos like the Oaks Club strongly protest this and maintain it is unfair to give them this advantage. I would expect that in the near future due to political pressure this limitation will change. In the meantime, the Oaks Club continues to thrive through its excellent organization and its good relationship with local and state officials. Gambling is under constant scrutiny because so much money and so many taxes are involved. The casino has to have transparent policies and open records so that outside auditors can review them. The Oaks Club bears a heavy financial burden of substantial taxes, health benefits, and insurance costs. All this necessitates a constant review of its administration, of profits and losses, and employee relations.

As stated before but which cannot be emphasized too much, the Oaks Club has been a family-owned business for almost one hundred years. Its stability over so long a time has had several notable consequences. First in its earliest development it had some competition but was in a strong position to counteract other gambling in Emeryville. Before 1920, there were about eighteen card rooms with which the Oaks Club had to contend. In more recent times, after 1970, there were still six surviving clubs but today there is only one, the Oaks Club. Secondly, a family-owned enterprise so locally situated has to be particularly aware of its reputation and heavily sensitive to the needs and desires of its patrons. And thirdly because of its ownership it has been able to attract and keep together a core of key managers. Five such managers have been with the casino an average of fifteen years or more. There is a kind of collegiality and cooperation among such employees that is unusual in any business. Furthermore, all the managers are visible and accessible to patrons. The owner functions as the chief executive officer as his father and grandfather were before him. He often roams about the casino, answers questions, knows regular players by their first names, and is clearly available to all his patrons. The same is true for the casino manager and the general manager.

There are usually one or more managers in each shift who observe dealers and players, settle disputes and in general try to keep tabs on what is going on around the clock in a large, crowded, and noisy card room. They too are familiar with regular players. In addition, some managers play poker irregularly which gives them a connection with players that enhances cordiality and their oversight.

The greatest contingent of employees are the dealers who number around one hundred and forty. A special manager is in charge of hiring, supervising, and firing dealers. He tries to evaluate their performances through observations and comments or complaints by patrons. His criteria for doing this is discussed in the chapter on dealers. However, it is an extremely demanding job that probably receives more complaints than praise. Dealers may have gripes about both managers and players. Players often complain about dealers and managers. All in all though, the supervision and performance has been run fairly well. There is, however, a fair amount of dealer turnover due to the competition from other casinos that complicates the staffing of dealers. Given low hourly wages and ready employment elsewhere, this is not unusual.

Players are not only interacting with dealers but, in addition, to a shift boss, floor monitors, chip persons, or those controlling or servicing the various poker tables. My experience has been that, in general, they perform their tasks very well. However, many interviewed regular players question the efficiency and quality of supervision and service. Several of them have very strong adverse views about the competency of both dealers and floor managers. The one complaint I have heard most often is that decisions over some disputes at the poker tables are not resolved quickly enough or even correctly to the satisfaction of players. Floor managers are visibly present but at times seem inattentive to what is going on. It is certainly not an easy management task but there is a consensus among many players that it could be done much better. For example, the person arranging the games makes mistakes such as wrongly removing a player's name from the reservation list, waiting too long to start a game when there is obviously a long list of potential players, and of not quickly filling empty seats in any card game. There are monitors on the floor that observe dealers. It is also surprising that sometimes these floor managers use the wrong rule to make a judgment or hesitate too long in making a decision. Nothing will irritate players more than such outcomes.

There are ten shift managers in all in the Oaks Club. California State law requires that at least one of them be on duty during each eight-hour shift. Above them are managers with special responsibilities such as supervising dealers, administering credit policies for players, and in organizing tournaments. There are a casino manager and general manager that oversee the entire gambling operation. The tournament manager has become increasingly important in meeting competition from other casinos and most of all for attracting players who might not otherwise come to the casino. There are over one hundred tournaments held in a year usually on daytime weekends and on a midweek evening. Depending upon how many poker players have signed up the winner may get up to $2,000. The popularity of tournaments, especially those promoted on television, underline how important they are to the profits and attractions for any casino.

Another major casino feature are what are called "jackpots." These are arrived at this way. First, in order to create a jackpot pool of money (i.e., $15,000) the dealer collects or "drops" one dollar from each winning pot. For a jackpot to occur one player must have aces full of tens or better be beaten by another player who has four of a kind. The major limitation is that the two players need to use both of their down cards in order to qualify. Jackpots now occur perhaps once or twice every two weeks where formerly because of lower requirements they took place at least once a week. Currently, at the Oaks Club, the "loser" will win about $7,000, his competitor about $3,000. The remaining dollars that are left in the pool are equally divided among the other players, amounting usually to $400 or $500 depending how many are in the game. In some other casinos, there are jackpots of $100,000 or more.

A particular responsibility for the Oaks Club is to keep a daily count of how many of its chips are in circulation in the casino. This requirement is mandated by California state law. One day while I was in the casino the chip count stood at 1,755,000 dollars and changed every day. Once a month someone makes an inventory of all chips in play at the various games. To this is added those that are in the cashier's office. Any shortages between what the casino should have and what it actually has must be covered by money in the casino's bank account.

Since money is what pays the bills and turns the wheels in a casino a competent credit manager and fair credit policies are absolutely essential. Huge amounts of cash are received and paid out daily. Personal checks are used by players who have established their good credit. As a policy casino check cashing is relatively easy once your account has been established. They have to submit a financial statement and have their bank accounts verified. Credit is much harder to obtain at the Oaks Club and is kept to minimum. Second party checks are not acceptable and the law requires that the casino cannot cash welfare or social security checks. The reasoning behind this requirement is quite clear—to supposedly prevent those who cannot afford to gamble from doing so. It is unclear whether such a policy is an actual deterrent. Many regular players who have established credit use what are called "markers" to buy chips. These markers are later submitted for cashing against a player's bank account. If the problems of the lack of funds or bad checks cannot be resolved the debt is turned over to a collection agency. However, the casino wants to avoid at all costs using such agencies, the police, or the courts. Litigation is an anathema to a casino. It is not only costly, often unproductive, and may permanently drive patrons away from the casino. I have been told that in most cases the Oaks Club would rather write-off bad debts than take any legal action. In this regard casino credit policies may seem too generous and forgiving compared to regular business practices. The casino, however, provides a strong incentive for players to pay up; it can bar them from its premises though usually not for more than two months. In one year the Oaks Club received only eight bad checks. The so-called "dead-beat" players will try to right their credit reputation and their delinquencies as quickly as possible. The casino credit system works well for itself and its patrons, another distinction from other businesses.

The present credit manager is also the casino manager and has been with the Oaks Club for over thirty years. Over this long period he has seen all the credit collection realities and player's excuses that one can imagine. His decisions are guided by knowing many individual patrons on a first-name basis and by referring to their credit history. He is usually on duty daily in the central gambling room; he is kind of a walking symbol that may remind players of their financial obligations. The downside of the casino's credit policy is that it makes it easier for patrons to play beyond their financial means with heavy consequences. After all, for some gambling is addictive with results unlike alcohol and drugs. In any case, it is clear that all poker players are on their own no matter casino policies.

This chapter has not been intended as an evaluation of the way in which the Oaks Club conducts its business. However, in describing things and using interviews it may appear that I have done so. This is unavoidable in looking at an institution as complex as a casino and as filled with so many activities. It may be clear that some things need changing or improvement, but I am not necessarily suggesting such. Rather it follows as a consequence of my observations or descriptions not my intent or purposes. In the gambling world players and dealers may be at odds with management. Management may overlook the justifiable complaints of their patrons and dealers. Judged by standards of longevity and profits the Oaks Club is doing well and is relatively open to suggestions about its policies. I have tried to highlight some of the ways in which this has been accomplished through the reactions of its clientele. Life's problems are similar; remedies vary. In any case, players such as myself have picked the Oaks Club in which to play because of convenience, a comfortable environment, fair treatment, and guaranteed poker action.

VII. Players: The Only Patrons of Poker

Clearly casinos need players but players do not need casinos. However, for the great majority of poker players the casino is where the action is. In home games you play with friends; the stakes are modest and you can play many different "wild" card games. Not so in a casino where mainly regular poker or a few other standard games are in order. Casinos are always open and a variety of low and high limits are offered. For me, players are by far the most interesting persons in a casino aside from being the most numerous. The two longest chapters in this book attest to this.

Seated around a casino poker table there is often an extraordinary diversity of clientele in terms of age, gender, ethnicity, personality, and past experience. Step into the Oaks Club at any time and you will find at one or more poker tables a veritable cross-section of the United States adult male population. There is no ethnic or social divide; seemingly everyone is represented. There are several factors associated with casinos such as the Oaks Club that attract this diverse clientele. First of all, casino gambling is open and routinely welcoming to all individuals Anyone can enter at any time. No membership, no entrance fee, no identity cards, and no credit references are required. Aside from the games its other activities are its bar, restaurant, and constant security. It is a congenial place in which to play or merely observe. Legal age of twenty-one years in California is the only requirement for entry and participation. A player who had won a jackpot was denied payment because he was underage. One can say that card games are part of a democratic activity where every player is valued, has an equal chance to win, and where the rules are clear and the same for everyone. A stranger can enter the Oaks Club as easily as a regular customer. It is easy to be in the casino and one can leave unnoticed. It is a semi-private world that one can be in without any commitment and leave at will without any farewells.

Men represent 95% or more of all poker players in the casino. On one sample day I counted only ten women playing in contrast to one hundred and eighty men. The number of female players is rising but their numbers are still small. However, more and more women know about poker from the various televised tournaments. In any mix of poker patrons diversity is obvious, particularly in their ages and occupations. At any table you might easily find young college students, middle-aged blue collar workers, and senior citizens. Ages can range in the Oaks Club from twenty-one to ninety years. There are about six or more regular poker players who are over eighty years of age. I have played with one retired person who had been gambling at the Oaks Club for more than fifty years. College students are dangerously trying to pay for their education. Many players regardless of their background have an obvious passion for poker and many old timers relish casinos. It provides many poker players with comfortable space to fill their empty time and give them some tame excitement.

A notable feature in this diversity are the various occupations of players I have encountered while playing. These are among many others the following: two chiropractors, several carpenters, a plumber, police persons, a taxicab driver, teachers, a chemist, an engineer, a deckhand, two house painters, a beautician, several mechanics, an organic farmer, a musician, a restaurateur, and many businessmen. The list could be added to, I am sure.

Some players appear in attire that immediately identifies them as with paint-stained overalls, businessmen in suits and ties, and bus drivers marked by their identification badges. There is certainly no dress code for casino poker players. One can see all kinds of clothing including printed T-shirts, colorful jackets with various logos, gloves, baseball caps, scarves, hoods, and sports clothing of all kinds. One chap who said that red was his lucky color showed me the red jockey shorts he always wore when playing! Many tattoos are in evidence. The best-dressed persons in the casino are the floor managers, some of whom must have the largest collection of gaudy ties in the world. It is not a fashion scene.

The most striking diversity among players are their ethnic backgrounds. The most noticeable are Asian Americans, of which Chinese constitute about 30% of all patrons. Indicative of this is that the only casino party for invited guests occurs during Chinese New year. There are also major representations of Filipino-Americans, Vietnamese, and Koreans. Add to this are many Latin Americans, Middle Easterners, and a very large group of African Americans. You can easily see how extraordinary is this diversity. Of course, the largest group can be broadly identified as white American males and those with various European backgrounds. There is a popular belief that one can determine the poker style of players by their ethnic background or race. As an example, it is purported that Chinese-Americans have a higher propensity to gamble than other groups. Of course, there is no scientific evidence to document such a contention. It should be noted that Chinese-Americans many times are the majority players in such casino games as pai gow, double-hand poker, and blackjack. Many players speak English as a second language that underscores the diversity among the casino's patrons. Some players are convinced that ethnicity matters and gender also makes a difference. Such attitudes still persist. Suffice it to say, these views are no different than those that one generally finds in the outside society.

There are also a variety of physical factors among players that have consequences for their participation. Vision and hearing are the most significant. Players with vision problems try to occupy seats in the middle of the table which enables them to see face-up cards better. Even in good seats accurately reading cards in one's hand or those that are exposed can be tricky. I have misread my hands and those cards that are on the table many times, though it may be due to a lack of my alertness than to vision. Hearing can also be a problem though most dealers will assist such players. Blindness is of course an absolute barrier given the nature of poker. Persons in wheelchairs can also be accommodated to enable them to play. Anyone can misread or miscalculate cards that are in play which may also have something to do with faulty memory or distraction. In any case, clearly obvious physical disabilities are usually tolerated by dealers and players. In addition, the casino because of the law must provide easy access for disabled persons.

Poker players are a strange breed and quite distinctive in the scheme of human behaviors. They exhibit a wide variety of personal mannerisms that relate to their play and the play of others in any given hand. Table talk among them is common and can be particularly expressive, even offensive, or merely simple conversation. They may indulge in puns, malaprops, oxymorons, and a variety of jokes. They may recommend movies, restaurants, and compare service to other casinos. There may be references to current events as well as stock market prices that flash on TV screens above the players. Many are prima donnas that at times are almost impossible to play with. Some players record their winnings and losses for a yearly accounting. A few players may selectively list many of the hands they have played over the course of a year. This is certainly not bookkeeping for tax purposes! Players are not supposed to talk about their cards or those of anybody else's during a hand but they often do so, requiring a reprimand from the dealer. Players are supposed to act in turn but often they do not. Players are not supposed to use their cell phones while at the table but they often do so. This is a major advantage for those who wish to play and conduct business at the same time. Some players read mysteries or the *Card Player* magazine or do crossword puzzles if they are not in hand but there are those who may do so during their play. Some players listen to music on their headphones which causes inattentiveness and delays the game. Some players divert their attention by joking or flirting with waitresses.

There are players who doze off or actually fall asleep having either spent far too many hours in the casino or having consumed too much alcohol. A few players are extremely slow in reacting when it is obviously their turn. It may be because of age or a preoccupation with their own hand or even a poker tactic to lull competition. Many poker players will look at their "hole" or down cards several times before play is completed. I have observed that a few players constantly do this four times or more. Nervous habit, an obsession, "pokerheimer," or a ploy, who knows?

Players have distinct ways of behaving or expressing themselves that are reflected in their spoken words, in body language, and in facial expressions. Some stroke their beards, twirl their mustaches, scratch their scalp, and make all sorts of arm and upper body gestures. Toothpicks protruding from their mouths are common and cigarettes and cigars as well though they can't light them. Astute players think they can detect or read habits that may tip-off an opponent's hand or recognize ahead of time who will call, check, raise, throw their hands away, or who are bluffing. There is a mystique about decoding or predicting another player's foibles or ploy. It is true that some players may give themselves away by being too nervous, especially when they are losing, bluffing, or have unbeatable hands. Experienced and watchful poker players note such things and try to use them to advantage. Good players will attempt to mask their play, particularly if they have a potentially winning hand or are bluffing. Such a strategy is often-used to check and raise. Some players deliberately take long pauses before acting or by calling "time" before they bet or call in order to vary their play. Regular players who are in the casino three or more times a week are often fully aware of each others' traits and predilections. Some players will check to see who their competitors will be before they enter a game. They are making a calculation based on their past experiences of these players as to who they do or do not prefer to play with. Decoding the behaviors of newcomers is more problematic. More volatile players will curse, pound the table, or throw their cards up in the air in frustration over losing or elation over winning. They may also use distasteful language directed to another player sometimes causing near-violence between them. Some players may be banned for a short time because of this. It may be for a day, a week, or in extremely rare cases for a much longer period. Typically, one may find there are usually one or two regular players at a table who at one time or another had been temporarily banned. Playing poker can sometimes bring out the worst in what are ordinarily nice persons.

We have noted that players exhibit all manner of irritating behaviors such as slow play, acting out of turn, and commenting on the hands of others. Arguments about presidents, war, peace, and taxes sometimes arise and get in the way of normal playing. Players must show both of their "hole" cards at the end of each hand unless they are the only one left. Particularly irritating is when the winner must show his hand and does it so slowly in what is called a "slow roll." It is as if the winner is mocking the losers or merely having fun at their failure. In any case it does not go down well with other players. A losing player is often offended if he is asked to show his hand. Embarrassment or what, I do not know.

Many players will change seats several times if they are not winning and they may do this three or four times to change their luck. A few players will change tables if they are losing or if they prefer to play with certain persons. Many believe that certain seats are luckier than others and will reserve them before a game starts. Heated arguments may arise over who is entitled to a particular seat. In addition, there may be testy encounters when a player feels he is being crowded by a player on either side of him. Here they are playing a game in which one can lose or win hundreds of dollars and yet they are quite picky about something so seemingly trivial as seating. Some players have favorite starting cards that they have won with in the past or that correspond to their birth dates or whatever. Some players will play cards that appeared in the previous hand in the hope that they will immediately come up again. Some players will beseech the dealer to deal them "good" cards as if they had the power to do so. However, these things rarely bring winning results to the players in question. Such beliefs and predilections defy card logic yet it is common to observe players using them over and over again in poker. Such are again the many convictions and superstitions that characterize many poker players. What a funny world they and I play in!

Peculiar and distinct mannerisms seem to be endless. Take, for example, players will call their hands with purposefully misleading words such as "one pair" when they have the top pair (two aces) which are clearly winners. They may also call "two pairs" when they have four cards of one kind. If the winning player is the only one left in the hand he is not required to show his cards and most do not, preferring to keep their hands a mystery for obvious reasons. However, some will glibly show one card that is unrelated to their win rather than the one that is responsible for it. This is a kind of "rubbing it in" behavior or merely a conventional jest. In any case, it occurs during a game quite often, sometimes elucidating sarcastic responses from other players. Another unusual development is that some players will go on what is called "tilt." It is used to describe the actions of a losing player who gets so frustrated that he will play poor or low percentage hands and bet aggressively. He is trying foolishly to make up his losses quickly which rarely occurs. Another form of this is called a "rush," that is, a player who wins two or more pots in succession thinks more will follow. His conviction is so strong that he may play any two cards, good or bad. If he doesn't win he will say, "My rush is over." There are a variety of ways in which players "check" their hands or pass. Perhaps the most common ones are hand signals including waving one finger, pointing all five fingers, or using their fists. Many of such movements by poker players appear to be a reflection of habit. Many players will call the hands of another player and say, "I know you got me beat" and as predicted lose. On the face of it, this is a puzzling contradiction. It justifies the prediction of a player who doesn't take his own sound advice.

A few players at a table will leave their seats to go outside and smoke. Smoking was commonly allowed in most casinos until recent years. Such players may miss a few hands and, more importantly, not share in a jackpot should it arise. It might be said that for them one addiction (smoking) temporarily may have taken precedence over another (gambling). Players take breaks for a trip to the restroom, to make telephone calls, to eat food, to stretch their legs, or to walk about to recover from their frustrations about losing. There are players who leave their chips where they are sitting and wander off to play a non-poker game in another part of the casino. This of course is not allowed but some do it anyway until they get caught. Some few players get slightly high or drunk usually on beer. Floor managers may order waitresses to stop serving them drinks, though this is seldom done. If a player missed three rounds of blinds his chips will be picked up and he will lose his seat at the table. Many players are at a table for several hours, some all day, and some hardy ones play continuously for twenty-four hours or more. One player with whom I shared a table had been playing for more than forty-eight hours. Needless to say, he had to be prodded from time to time to keep him from falling asleep. I do not know what the record is but I have heard about individuals who played for four or five days! Some players are involved in far too many hands; they seem to not be out of any pot no matter how poor their cards. During a three-hour period I observed one player who played in eighty-six hands out of a possible ninety-eight and only won eight times. These are phenomenal numbers for one player when conventional wisdom says you should play no more than 35% of all hands. However, such are the vagaries of some gamblers. Players may be involved in eating, listening to music, talking on cell phones, and gazing up at television screens. These generally are only minor distractions. In some players there is a kind of adrenaline flowing that keeps them reasonably alert and enables them to sustain a reasonable quality of play. Also a player who has won a jackpot or other large amount gains instant notoriety or recognition from many regulars who will offer congratulations. Player gossiping in the casino is quite common. In any case fame, however, is fleeting and tomorrow merely starts another day.

Experience is a prime factor in the success or failure of many poker players. It provides a long-time player with card knowledge and with the ability at times to anticipate or judge the hands of competitors because he has done this many times before. Many players are trying to assess a loser's or winner's hand by asking questions of them which are usually ignored or lied about. Patience and confidence are important attributes of all good players. A large amount of chips that a player has will give him a useful advantage. What counts in poker is not so much a player's expertise but how he uses it. Being a good poker player is not synonymous with being a successful gambler. Most players judge themselves on how much money they have won no matter how fleeting their rewards. Some players will tell you in the course of a game how much they are "out" or losing. Hardly any will tell you how much they are winning. I don't know why this is so. Perhaps winners are leery of the Internal Revenue Service. Income from gambling is taxable; not to divulge it is standard practice. For gamblers the risk is small and the joy of deceiving the government is great. Poker players feel they are entitled to win and to keep it all. I tend to judge players not just on their wins but how gracefully and wisely they lose. I suppose this view is part of my romantic disposition.

Poker players make mistakes just like any of us. The difference is that they must pay for them instantly. Below is a listing of some typical mistakes that I have observed over time and provide insights to the hazards of playing poker, in this case, Texas Hold'em. They are as follows:

1.   Misreading the value of your cards that cost you a certain win;

2.   Accidentally exposing your cards;

3. Inadvertently throwing your cards face down into the so-called "muck" so that they cannot be retrieved, costing you a win;

4. Unknowingly throwing a winning hand away;

5. Waiting for a particular card to come up that would make you a winner but another card appears instead. You are so intent on missing the card you wanted that you overlook a different card that also would have made you a winner.

Some players are an enigma and play illogically which makes poker both interesting and challenging. Poker requires what players call the "smarts." Intuition, hunches, and bluffing are sometimes more effective than the best playing strategies. Some players have what amounts to an obsession for raising the pot no matter the value of their cards. Though it enlivens the game it is a recipe for losing. Always lurking around all poker rewards or failures are chance and luck which no player can control or foresee. These are humbling variables but they contribute fascination to the game of poker. Poker players can be characterized as heroes, adventurers, crooks, cranks, actors, egotists, optimists, entrepreneurs, scoundrels, simpletons, jokers, gentlemen, or a combination of them. There is no logic in such a variety; membership in these categories requires no fee, no references, and confers no favors. Just bring yourself and your money; the casino will provide the rest. In an April 2005 edition of the *New Yorker Magazine*, there is a cartoon showing two men dressed in formal business suits and carrying briefcases. They are clearly brokers or investment managers. One of them says to the other, "Right now all my money is in poker." Good luck to you and, of course, to me!

VIII. Players: You, Me, and They

Poker books are full of stories about professional players and their widely advertised and supposedly great achievements. My poker world in contrast is filled with ordinary amateur players whose personalities and the anecdotes about them are to me as equally interesting as those of big-time gamblers. Average players never make headlines and never appear in books. Many of them, however, are serious students of poker that discuss with each other hands played and faithfully watch and analyze televised tournaments. They all have engaging habits, notable idiosyncrasies, varied backgrounds, and personal styles that are just as intriguing as those of their professional counterparts. This chapter presents and describes some such players in their casino context—and they will be only those with whom I have actually played in the Oaks Club.

I have selected fourteen examples of various players for description which hopefully will highlight their individuality and say something as well about the characteristics of players in general. I have briefly interviewed all of them and have observed their behavior in the casino on and off for ten years or more. These players are not presented as either prototypes or stereotypes. I have mixed styles and personalities among them so they cannot be easily identified. However, I am sure some will recognize themselves. Most players seek anonymity; some seek attention. We all can be winners and losers. I have selected mostly those who play regularly at the Oaks Club and play Texas Hold'em. Surprisingly, they have been quite forthcoming with me in answering questions about the games, competitors, dealers, and management.

Players can be described and studied as social individuals as well as contestants in gambling, noting their distinct personalities and varying styles of play. Players can be outspoken or taciturn, aggressive or laid back, crafty or naïve, and zany or sane. I have been told of one player who bet twice without any cards in his hand. And another who briefly fainted, ended up on a stretcher and on his way out he was heard to say, "Keep me on the list for the 6/12 game." Perhaps he made it, perhaps not. One player was arrested by the FBI but he was allowed to cash in his chips before he was handcuffed and carted off. They can be viewed as amateur actors performing on a crowded stage without scripts and with many unexpected interventions. Some are akin to being "graduates" of acting schools so pronounced are their sometimes deceptive ways. Their behaviors may be generally predictable, their actual hands not so. Players clearly are the only real and important characters in poker. Their peculiarities enliven the game as if they were entertainers in the human comedy of competitive life. I describe them here so that they and others may share my experience. Other poker players can compare them to their own or merely enjoy their descriptions.

The first player is a white, middle-aged male who talks constantly during the course of a game. Silence to him is akin to being asleep. There are no comments that are beyond him including off-color jokes, bad beat stories, judging the play of others, and remarking about any manner of things. He is a fairly good player as well as a raconteur but presumes that he is an expert in all poker matters. Chance, luck and illogical plays of others are his enemies. His Achilles heel are players who win with poor hands. He is an active competitor quick to jump on any infringement of the rules. He acts as a self-appointed captain of the table, incurring the irritation of other players.

The second is a thirty-five-year-old white male who plays poker only as a challenge to win and says confidently that he has "beaten" the game. He is particularly angered by any rule infractions no matter how trivial. He generally holds many dealers in low regard because he expects them to perform mistake-free which, according to him, most do not do. He takes breaks to smoke, often changes his seat, and has a general disdain for players he deems inferior. He has his own private standard for judging the play of others and tends to regard competition as potential prey. He is often considered a regular complainer by management.

My third example is a white male in his early forties who loves to talk loudly, gestures with his hands and head, and at times is both sarcastic and affable. On one occasion he was barred from the casino because of his verbal abusiveness. His temperament can be an albatross that causes him defeats. He eats breakfast in the afternoon and at times drinks too much. He is always beseeching that good cards turn up for him. He is surprisingly easily resigned to losing but takes up a lot of psychological space at the table.

A fourth player is a Chinese-American male in his twenties with a flair for aggressive betting. He will sometimes decide to raise many hands in succession even though his cards may not warrant it. At times after he loses he will also bang his hand on the table to emphasize his frustration. He is often reprimanded for speaking Chinese rather than English to a friend at the table. This is prohibited under casino rules because such a language cannot be understood by other players who are non-speakers. He appears to be wealthy, is unperturbed by losses, and loves to check and raise. He never eats or drinks while playing. He often will play for one or two days in succession. He will always keep at least $400 worth of chips with which to play so he never has to resort to being "all-in," that is, being short of chips to cover all bets.

Out fifth candidate is a fifty-year-old Filipino-American who has a stern facial expression, rarely talks, and seems not to know the relative value of hands. He will at times speak Tagalog rather than English. He checks his hands with one finger, a movement which is so slow that it is not easily noticed by other players. This latter seems merely to be a habit not a strategic ploy. He either stares at other players or completely ignores them. To me he is an enigma.

A sixth example is a seventy-year-old white male with a fine beard and mustache who has played poker for more than forty years, much of it at the Oaks Club. He is notably courteous to other players, jokes pleasantly, and has a genial way of playing. He will often just shrug his shoulders when accepting the fact of his losing cards. He will make a benign comment such as, "Oh, well." He wears an Oakland Raiders football cap, among others, plays almost every day, and knows the game of poker well. He is one of the most pleasant players with whom I have shared a poker table.

Our seventh player is a forty-seven-year-old white male, a former surveyor and a poker know-it-all. He will bet or raise with any two picture cards, but is generally otherwise conservative in playing. He is very talkative and attracts both negative and positive attention from other players. He virtually loves to tell jokes; he is a walking encyclopedia of them, both dirty and polite. He can be quite provocative and sometimes comes perilously close to heated arguments with other players.

An eighth example is someone who should not be playing poker at all. He seems not to know the relative value of his cards or when to bet, raise, or call. He is infatuated with any pair in his hand, no matter how small. He is overweight, usually unshaven, and with an attire that appears to indicate that he just got out of bed. One of his peculiar and obsessive habits is writing down in a small notebook everything that takes place in a hand. This notebook is full of seemingly indecipherable scribbles and diagrams. He writes in it surreptitiously so that supposedly no one can see what he is recording. He is simply a very poor player and constant scribbling does not improve his play. He invokes my disdain, not my sympathy. Fortunately, he has been absent from the Oaks Club for a long time, perhaps convinced he would have more success at bingo or the racetrack.

I trust you are not getting weary of any of this succession of types of poker players. In any case, here is another one and one of my past favorites. He is a grouchy seventy-five-year-old man who played regularly and was formerly a baker in the Merchant Marine. When you greeted him with a "good morning," his response in a gruff, dismissive manner usually was, "What's good about it!" He played poorly and had an extreme obsession for checking and raising. A memorable example was a hand in which he had two queens and two of the three flop cards were also queens. He had practically what is called the "nuts," an unbeatable hand of four queens. He was in the first betting position but merely checked as did all the players behind him. The two remaining cards on the table were turned up and still with four queens he checked again. He was anxiously waiting for someone else to bet so he could raise. He never got the opportunity, everyone checked and the hand was over. Our baker won ten dollars which could have been much more had he done something besides waiting to raise. He was also not obverse to cheating when he thought he had a potentially winning hand. He would take chips from his pocket and increase his stack after he had seen his cards. This, of course, was prohibited. He did it one time when he held two kings and the flop was another king. Suddenly he slyly removed from his pocket several yellow (five-dollar) chips. He had other competitors in the hand, one of whom held two aces and a flop of one ace. The old man now had three kings but his opponent had three aces. Several of us had seen what our grump had done with chips but said nothing until the hand was over. His three kings were beaten by three aces so he lost all his money including the extra illegal chips. We all laughed and if there ever was anyone who deserved to be "foisted on his own petard," it was he. No one mentioned his chicanery since he got what he deserved. His ploy in both cases was so ludicrous that it was only believable if you were there to witness it. When he learned I often traveled to Indonesia he began to call me "Jungle Jim." He could not imagine there was any civilization in a country like this. One occasion he surprisingly offered to lend me money to keep me in the game. It was a rare but most appreciated gesture from him. Despite his transparent dishonesty and his other shenanigans, he was an endearing character that I will always remember. He passed away probably mumbling as he always did when he was playing. To this day many of us still talk about the old curmudgeon and his two memorable hands.

Our next player is an attractive female in her early thirties. She comes to the Oaks Club irregularly but when she does she attracts a great deal of attention from men. She dresses colorfully and provocatively—a short skirt and a tight sweater. She is friendly, alert, confident, and a relatively good player. However, I expect that she commands attention due to her sexiness and attire rather than to her poker tactics. She does not stay long in the casino, quits when she is ahead, and in many respects is not a typical reticent female player.

The most inscrutable poker player I have ever met is a tall, handsome black male about forty-five years old. He is a super serious player, very self-confident, and entirely focused on the game. His basic strategy was to bet or raise aggressively when he had any semblance of a good hand. His style of play often included bluffing, but it was hard to determine when he was doing this. He hardly uttered a word during play and when he said, "check" or "raise" it was barely audible. He never played too long and appeared to be playing in between periods of regular work. He never seemed neither relaxed or nervous. His behavior and play have been always puzzling to me.

Perhaps my favorite player was a sixty-five-year-old white male who was a retired petroleum engineer. He had learned to play poker the hard way in sleazy Louisiana card rooms and on oil rigs in the Gulf of Mexico. He sometimes recounted stories about poker players who carried guns and oil workers who brawled. He was a quiet, good-natured, and highly experienced poker player. He usually played four or five times a week. He was quite adept at "slow playing" his potentially winning hand so that others did the betting for him while he collected all the chips at the end. I usually sat next to him and he often commented sarcastically about my playing cards which he regarded as poor or mediocre. We often "potted" for lunch, that is, which one of us won the first pot would have to pay for it. Since I played many more hands than him I often ended up paying for his lunch. One day while playing he was forced to leave the casino because of dizziness and pain. He could just barely drive home. Later we learned he had a terminal brain tumor. Another player and I visited him at his home just before he passed away. I sadly remember him saying to me, "Joe, my game is over." I shall always have fond memories of playing with him.

The most animated of all players that I played poker with was a fifty-five-year-old white male. His large rotund body rested uncomfortably on his seat and he seemed always on the verge of falling off. He was flamboyant and had an instant comeback remark to anything that was said at the table that bothered him. He had a Middle Eastern first name and at times recited semi-religious words of wisdom that he obviously had made up. He was our candidate for life-of-the-party. My clearest recollection of him involved a jackpot hand in which I won several thousand dollars and all the seated players shared lesser sums. However, just before this our unlucky chap had gone to the restroom. When he returned the jackpot hand was over but you had to have been seated to win anything; this cost him about $500. Out of my poker compassion I gave him $100 of my own money. He never forgot the gesture. After that he still came often to the casino but was clearly showing signs of a serious illness. He had lost all his hair and was under treatment for cancer yet he was still his old upbeat self. He died sometime later; another one of my enjoyable poker chums was gone.

The most physically striking player that I have met was a forty-year-old burly Pacific Islander who looked the size of a whale. Like a whale he was constantly spouting, usually with caustic and inappropriate comments. He would utter phrases like, "Your hand isn't worth shit," or "I am going to get you" or "Don't mess with me" and so on. This kind of talk for him was more like a habit rather than an intended personal insult. He loved to check and raise and his colorful invectives became for me part of his allure. He was certainly a commanding as well as an entertaining presence. Despite his gruff behavior he was tolerated and even liked by other players. It is as if he was a big dramatic performer on a stage with an audience who he knew would pay attention to him and he reveled in this. I had a fantasy that he sailed the Pacific ocean in an ancient outrigger, catching large fish, and gambling his wages away in his spare time in some island saloon. I have not now seen him very often so I haven't been able to ask if any of my conjecture was true.

Then there is a player who seems to play around the clock. He often dozes while playing. He is often paged on the telephone but never answers it. One day after many unanswered telephone calls his angry wife appeared in the casino, placed her baby on the table in front of her husband, and left! This may be one of the reasons that players just use first names or pseudonyms. Many clearly wish to remain anonymous while gambling lest they be discovered by their spouses.

And finally there is me, who is a poker player I have known intimately for more than seventy years. I am a seventy-nine-year-old white male. I was a university teacher and some players call me the "Professor," a label which continues whether my play is expert or bad. This is a kind of grudging appellation which has little to do with the quality of my poker playing, but it may be a response to my taking notes for this book. Scribbles attract attention. It reflects the monikers that players often like to pin on some of their compatriots or themselves. I have heard others with similar "tags" such as the Commandant, One-thousand and one, Seven-and-Two, CFN, ABC, XYZ, ZYX, Dad, the Rack Man, OSB or One-Stack-Bob, G-Man, Playboy, Ice, Beaver (referring to an Oregon football team), the Kid, and the Wild Man. On occasion I forget to bring enough money with which to play and borrow from a player I know well. The appellation "Absent-minded Professor" adds to my notoriety! One thing that gets me a reputation for unreasonable play is my seeming obsession for mediocre cards. So much so, in fact, that when low cards (a seven, eight, etc.) turn up some may call them "Joe" cards. I will admit that if both of my small down cards are suited or are sequential my temptation to play them is great. And I often give in despite poker logic. The attraction is winning with cards no matter how poor or low, and I am elated when I do so. It is as if something in me rises up from the ashes of poker to defeat a better player who holds superior cards; the underdog "gloriously" prevails. I will often lament if it turns out that the cards I threw away turned up winners. Some would call what I do a reflection of adverse "senior moments" or he is getting too old to play well. I have tried to give up this style but more often than not the temptation is still great. My poker brain is sometimes governed by emotion rather than reason—and of course other players do not mind this at all.

In every poker game there is another less obvious game going on at the same time. This "game" may be just as important as the cards you are holding or the chips that you are betting. It involves observing the style and traits of other players. Some wish to mask their play and demeanor; others like myself often reveal themselves. For both types a bit of so-called "play acting" may be apparent, not dissimilar to what goes on in social life in the outside world. Most players observe others who in turn are also observed. This underscores some interesting verities and varieties of human behavior in a game called poker. I have presented these fourteen examples of poker players precisely to demonstrate them. And I am sure there are many more interesting and colorful types out there.

And finally I conclude this chapter with a poker player I have yet to meet and probably never will. He is experienced, relatively skillful, never delays the game, and always plays in turn. He is mildly sociable but not too talkative. He never tells "bad beat" stories or off-color jokes. He doesn't wear headphones to listen to music and he leaves the table if his cell phone rings. He never eats or drinks while playing. He varies his play so as not to be predictable. He always keeps within his financial limits and knows when to leave when his winnings are sufficient or his losses too great. He rarely criticizes how others play and never raises questions except about obvious rule infractions. Dealers like him because he tips adequately and leaves them to run the game.

He never lets poker interfere with his regular life and does not hide from anyone the fact that he likes to gamble. Is there such a player somewhere? I doubt it and, in any case, he might be a big bore. I don't expect to ever find a perfect poker player but if you know one let me know. I would like to meet and interview him in person.

I have had, as I said, first-hand experiences with all the players I described. Some I detested, some I liked, and some I ignored. You no doubt can detect who are my favorites and who were not. Your fellow players are supposedly anonymous yet over time you develop knowledge and strong feelings about some of them. There is a certain social intimacy, no matter how fleeting or seemingly superficial, among players sitting at the same poker table. When one of the regular players is absent for a long time you wonder what has happened to him. Is he ill, passed on, gone to jail, moved away, squandered all his money, lost his job, or merely given up gambling? Many players that I have known have disappeared without my knowing what happened to them. It is an empty and sad feeling for me to have been "so close" to a player for so long a time and only know that they are missing.

IX. Dealers: Clerks in the House of Cards

Dealers are clearly the most essential personnel in running a casino poker game. They above all others have the most direct and continuing contact with players. Dealers maintain and enforce most of the established casino playing rules and settle minor disputes. Despite this it is surprising that they receive only minimum hourly pay which makes their hourly wages the lowest in casinos. (The principal source of their income is tipping which is discussed later.) Their overall performance, their attitude toward patrons, and how reliably they run a game are criteria for evaluation used by both players and management. Old and new dealers have been kept on or hired because of certain qualifications. These include past and present references and experience, knowledge of poker; language, communication, mathematical abilities and their sociability.

In the Oaks Club there are from one hundred to two hundred dealers in the employer's pool. They work eight-hour shifts day or night. Fifty percent of their hourly wage can be paid for overtime, providing they work no more than two hours. Their minimum hourly pay fixed by California state law is at this writing six dollars seventy-five cents. Tips can represent fifty percent of what they earn daily. By agreement with the Internal Revenue Service a fixed rate is assessed and collected daily by the casino on their tips. Despite their low wages and the uncertainty of income from tips, dealers enjoy a number of benefits which workers in general do not have. Depending on seniority, dealers can choose the shifts they prefer and also change them for good reason.

They can also opt for a two-hour shift if there are plenty of fulltime dealers available. They also can be called upon voluntarily to "float" if they are present in the casino but are not part of a regular shift in order to fill in if needed. It appears that schedules for dealers are flexible and can take into account their individual needs. They also can receive what are called "easy outs," which means they can leave their shifts for any good reason. Dealers can often take extra time off because there is usually a pool of others ready to step in or who are formally on-call. These options do not in any way adversely affect their continued employment unless they are repeatedly misused or otherwise unwarranted. These working conditions plus customary health benefits help offset their minimum hourly pay. And aside from managers, dealers in all earn the most money among casino employees. Unlike waitresses, cooks, and bartenders, there are no union contracts covering dealers. In some sense this gives dealers less bargaining power with management to affect policies, protect their jobs, or register complaints. The turnover among dealers is high. However the Oaks Club has several dealers who have worked there ten years or more. Turnover is generally due to competing casinos, some of which present better opportunities for higher earnings. Dealer firings by the Oaks Club are uncommon though many on trial are let go because of obvious deficiencies. Some few regular players have felt that there are at one time or another too many incompetent dealers whose questionable work is well known by management. They may be kept on due to management's loyalty over time, their personal connections or their backgrounds. Such factors for retaining workers are not dissimilar from those in any business. However, given the primary importance of dealers in poker it would seem that casino management should have a low tolerance for incompetence or failure. Whether in the case of this casino they do or not is an open question but often answered in the negative by many regular players.

Dealing is in sharp contrast to some other types of employment where seniority, expertise, upward mobility opportunities and union representation are incentives for job security, quality performance or financial success. However, as has been pointed out, dealers get rewarded by keeping their jobs, by following casino policies, by having flexible work schedules, by being popular with players, and by receiving tips which can be especially large if they deal a jackpot. They receive health benefits that are customary in the work world. After a limited time they are entitled to four weeks of paid vacation and six days sick leave.

There are always persons applying to be dealers at the Oaks Club. Prospective dealers who meet criteria for employment can be part of a training program organized by the casino. There is instruction in various casino card games and particular attention is paid on how dealers should run a game according to casino policies. If there are persons whose English and mathematics are inadequate they may be encouraged to improve themselves and later reapply to the casino. Training sessions are no small matter, for some applicants have never played poker, a background which often limits their becoming a good dealer. New dealers are employed for a trial period and are evaluated before they are offered a regular position. There appears to be no shortage of applicants but they far exceed the number who will qualify. All the dealers are responsible to a special manager who hires, supervises, and grades them. He also has to deal with their disputes, complaints about them, and respond to their individual or special needs. He is one of the most important managers in the Oaks Club because he is in charge of the largest number of employees.

Dealers are on the "front lines," so to speak, of poker. They are expected to handle disputes with players but they are told at the same time to "dummy up" and call floor managers to make many decisions. Their power to absolutely enforce all the casino rules is thus limited and makes running a game much harder. For example, unruly players will not be removed by management unless their behavior is extremely egregious. The stress on some dealers is apparent because they have to stay put at one table for at least a half an hour. They have to constantly guard against making mistakes and be alert to players' tricks and bad habits—and, on top of it all, be good natured. A standard response of dealers when they are wrongly criticized by players is to say, "I am only doing my job." Dealers have learned, as some put it, not to "take home" their unpleasant casino experiences. Most dealers, however, have developed workable and acceptable ways to relate to and tolerate players in the casino environment. However, some may be short-tempered and non-communicative. Despite standard casino rules and training sessions dealers exhibit extraordinarily different ways of running a game. Some also play poker as well as deal which enhances their relationships and knowledge of players. It somewhat ironic that dealers are required to wear dull shirts and black vests and ties. This makes them appear more like morticians or waiters. It is a traditional attire for service not command. Only during the month of December are they allowed to wear some colorful shirts.

The composition of the dealer corps is just as diverse in age, experience, and ethnic background as the players. The one exception is gender where there is a much higher proportion of women who deal compared to them as players. I am not sure why this is but it is clearly so. There are white Americans from various backgrounds, a large number of Chinese-Americans, many Filipino-Americans, as well as Latin Americans, Vietnamese, and Koreans. Some dealers have noticeable accents, which at times interferes with communication. Some have a poor comprehension of English, particularly in poker usage. These are disquieting factors in the hubbub of the casino. Some players feel strongly about this and are not reluctant to say so.

There is a lively social and psychological scene in which dealers are interacting with ten sitting players around a nine-foot table in the midst of an enormous central room. There is a kind of semi-superficial social atmosphere and even intimacy present. Dealers also know players by their first names, especially if they play regularly. Dealers will almost always recognize newcomers. Verbal exchanges between dealers and players are constant. It may consist of joking, straightforward card talk, and arguments over play. These exchanges at times can be heated;

players are not shy to, rightly or wrongly, criticize dealers especially when they are losing. Dealers have their favorite and least favorite players. Some players prefer certain dealers who supposedly bring them "luck" or disdain for those who do not. You often hear remarks from players such as "You haven't dealt me a winner in a month," or "Bring on another dealer." Players seem ardently to believe that dealers have the "power" to influence outcomes. The poker world is full of such beliefs or call them superstitions. Some dealers have personalities that fit into the game and some do not. There is among them a diversity of ways in which they deal and run a game. Some dealers are easily upset; some are totally in control. Remember the behavior and performance of dealers are open for all to see—and cannot be hidden. If a dealer is too much of a prima donna he or she will not last long in the job. The atmosphere around a table can really affect dealers. Some hardly respond to players while others are quick to do so. All dealers are subject to a variety of problems and difficulties. Dealers make mistakes just like players but the consequences are instant and they may affect all the players at the table, not just one. In addition, a few dealers appear reluctant to say, "I'm sorry," or apologize for their mistakes. Some of the more common dealer errors are:

1. Giving only one card to a player when it is supposed to be two or missing him altogether.

2. Turn a "burn" card too soon or a face-up card prematurely.

3. Miscalling a player's hand at the end of play.

4. Not seeing that players often act out of turn.

5. Mucking a player's hand by mistake, particularly those that sit to the immediate right or left of the dealer.

6. Dealing too many cards to any player.

7. Too tolerant of or too quickly to anger at a player's bad behavior.

8. Many dealers do not control the game by not indicating whose turn is next, who has bet, called or raised, or how many players are still in the hand.

They are targets for verbal insults and criticisms for making mistakes. Some losers have thrown cards at them. Two male dealers told me that one of the male players tried to kiss them. One player was drunk but the other was quite serious. Of course, the dealers resisted. Dealers are advised to be almost mute when problems arise and call for floor managers to solve them. Dealers can never satisfy all the expectations of such a diversity of players but some come very close to doing so. Clearly there are different annoyances on both sides. However, it is dealers that bear the brunt of "slings and arrows" which may only be offset by tips and "thank yous." Dealing is an exposed occupation that requires consistency, alertness, emotional control, affability, stamina, and who knows what else. Count me out!

X. Tipping: Convention and Generosity

Tips are by far the largest part of any dealer's income. Tips by definition are voluntary but most players simply automatically comply. It is a convention and a courtesy that appears unrelated to the quality of dealing or to the outcomes of a player. It is surprising that most often the size of a pot or even the stakes of a particular game have little or no effect on the amount of tip. One dollar and two dollar tips are standard for most of the Texas Hold'em games. This is a very small amount considering the winner's pot can amount to hundreds of dollars. A few players are more generous, especially if they are also dealers. Players may tip dealers that they are not fond of but they do no different to those who they like. A frustrated player may say, "No more tips from me," which is a kind of sarcastic jest. It is only when there is a jackpot that dealers receive any significant amounts of money as tips. Most players would probably be embarrassed if they did not tip dealers and this would be noticed disapprovingly by most of them. I have only heard one player who objected to tipping on principle, saying it amounted to a fee for playing. Players who never tip are rare and are well-known to dealers, still any action against them is not possible. If you consider tipping as not only a required convention but as a form of generosity, it emphasizes in part the social nature of some aspects in the game of poker. In this sense both dealers and players are socially connected to each other through tipping. The downside of minimal tipping is that it removes some incentive for dealers to improve their performance. Tipping is not considered by players as a reward for good service. Tipping is a kind of offering or handout not unlike those made by parishioners in church. Neither dealers nor churches can survive without them.

Each dealer keeps his or her own tips; they are not shared as is the practice of waitresses in many restaurants. In the Oaks Club, a standing agreement is in effect with the Internal Revenue Service that regulates the tax on income from the tips of dealers. All dealers are subject to an average eleven-percent tax regardless of the size of their daily earnings in tips. Dealers are strongly opposed to sharing tips and are zealously committed to maintaining their fair level of income at reasonable taxation rates. Tipping is a distinctive and constant feature in gambling casinos where dealers receive minimum hourly pay rather than weekly wages. It is one of those striking customs that characterize the playing of poker in casinos.

XI. Props: a Supporting Cast

Props are casino employees whose main task is to help start games that otherwise would not have enough participants with which to begin. They are also important in playing in so-called "short-handed" games for which there are not enough replacements and which are in danger of "breaking up." They are literally "propping up" beginning and ongoing games. They fill in and play until such time as there are enough regular players to replace them. Normally the casino likes to have five or six props available, many of whom are needed throughout the day. Players do not like "short-handed" games and prefer full tables of ten players. In addition there can be no jackpot unless there are at least six seated players. Some players do not like to play with props because they are considered too conservative and because they never stay long in any one game. Props may be required to play in any of the poker games but they are not obliged to do so in the higher limit games such as 15/30. Props can be called upon to play in many different games in a given day, switching from one game to another as is required. They may play Texas Hold'em, Omaha, Seven-card Stud, lowball, and pan. When not on duty they may play poker for themselves but not as employees. It is clear that props need to have considerable poker expertise to play in a variety of games during an eight-hour work shift. It suggests that they play continuously and patiently lest they lose more than their daily pay. Their losses are not protected; their wins obviously not guaranteed.

Props receive wages rather than hourly pay. Some of their earnings end up as a reimbursement which lessens the amount of their income tax. It is typical for props to be always on call when they are working in a regular day or night shift. A lot of their time is spent in waiting around and they can often be seen reading books or newspapers, watching television, or chatting with patrons. Props have clearly come to terms with idleness which am sure at times is a real bore. Low key behavior necessarily marks their personalities and style of play. They are a distinct group of employees that occupy a middle place between dealers and ordinary players. Over the years I have not seen much turn-over among props; they are filling a niche that the casino needs and within which most of them appear comfortable. Some props were formerly players who made the transition to employees. They are substitute players who in the best sense contribute to smoothly organized and run casino poker games.

XII. Cards and Table Talk

Casinos use special almost indestructible decks of cards which have closely drawn geometric designs on their backs. Two decks are in use in each poker game, one during the dealing while the other lies hidden inside an automatic shuffling machine that is embedded in the middle of the table. Dealers no longer have to shuffle cards which means about four to five more hands are dealt each round compared to those before the device was used. Random shuffling of cards theoretically takes place with the use of this machine. The plastic cards are replaced every four hours or so to prevent heat damage. They can also be washed and used again. In 1971 similar decks cost the casinos $4.00 each; it is $19.00. this is a considerable expense since the casino may use upwards of one thousand decks every month or so.

The heraldic or other designs on playing cards have changed very little since their origins in medieval times. This is particularly true of the "picture cards"; that is, kings, queens, and jacks. Cards aside from their specific use have varying connotations outside the game. For example, the highest card in a deck is an ace but in common parlance it is employed in such phrases as "having an ace in the hole," meaning a hidden source or opportunity for success in either life or cards. "Being within an ace" can mean you almost won something or that you had a narrow escape. Students may use the phrase, "I aced my exam," meaning they successfully passed it. These various phrases centered on the word 'ace" are used in business, personal life, and as noted in gambling.

The king card has the second highest ranking in poker. However, it is also commonly referred to in such phrases as "king of the hill" and "king of all he surveys." The king, of course, is an important chess piece which indicates defeat or triumph if you can capture it. The queen is the third highest card. It may be as the king associated with royal rules but in contrast is the most powerful piece in chess. The jack is the lowest of the picture cards. Its name is supposedly derived from the English ruler, John III, but the connection is unclear. In olden times it was called a knave which now commonly means an unprincipled or crafty man. It has meanings besides that of a jack in a deck of cards. Some are related to these of money or "jack" in words such as "jack it up" or raise the bet and in "hitting the jackpot" or reaping a great reward which has the same meaning in poker that is has in ordinary usage. One present term for it is the "hook" after the "J" which looks like a fishhook. It is also used as an appellation in terms "jack of all trades," lumberjack, steeplejack, and Jack Tar (sailor) and so on. The terms aces, kings, queens, and jacks in common usage appear to have only some modest connection to their value or usage in card games.

In Texas Hold'em cards in combination of five are called hands. Poker hands and individual cards have acquired over time an extraordinary number of special meanings. Some are colorful nicknames; some are associated with history and many have a folkloric quality. They are all a part of a specific poker language commonly used by professionals and amateurs alike. They are relatively unintelligible to non-poker players. They constitute a special and intriguing language heard wherever poker is played and, particularly, in casinos. This language and its uses may vary in different sections of the United States but their commonplace meanings are widespread. It is a kind of amazing and constantly growing gaming lingua franca. Those presented below are hardly an exhaustive number. The origins of these poker terms and phrases are difficult to trace and I have not added much to their history which might just be as interesting as how they are used in poker. In this book they all come from my hearing them from players, dealers, and managers in one casino, the Oaks Club, for over twenty-five years.

Readers are welcome to send me others or add to what I have described.

First, listed below are individual words that have specific and certain meanings for poker players. It is a glossary of special poker terms. These are as follows:

1. American Airlines or two aces, also pocket rockets, aces wired, or a pair of bullets.

2. Three nickels, signifying three fives; thirty miles or three tens.

3. Big Slick, an ace and a king as private down cards.

4. Huey, Duey and Louie or three deuces, a term which somehow comes from Donald Duck's nephews.

5. Dolly Partons or a pair of eights, referring to her ample breasts; also Oldsmobile 88.

6. Oregon Aces or a two and a three off-suit, one of the worst hands you can have.

7. Dead Man's hand or two aces and two eights, supposedly held by Wild Bill Hickok when he was shot in the back.

8. Canine, a king and a nine of cards.

9. Lamar or a seven and a four, named after the man who won a big and famous tournament with such poor cards.

10. Devil's Hand or three sixes and its connection to the anti-Christ.

11. Gay Waiter or a queen and a three (pronounced "tray"), a kind of sexual innuendo.

12. Bicycle, a straight composed of an ace and four of the next sequential cards (i.e., two, three, four, and five).

13. Dead Hand, one which cannot be used because of a mixed deal or other mistakes which disqualify it.

14. Rainbow, meaning all four suits are represented in the common or face-up cards.

15. Snowman, a player who bluffs a lot; often the verb form is used, i.e., "snowing."

16. Chip-burner, a player who continually bets aggressively with mediocre hands and usually loses.

17. Cowboy, an aggressive player.

18. Muck or cards already discarded in the center of the table, used as a verb (i.e., "mucked") to indicate a player who has thrown his cards away.

19. Flop, the first three cards turned up.

20. Flop lag, face cards that would have made a winner for someone in the previous hand.

21. Kicker, a significant secondary or high card that often determines which hand when tied will win, derived from the word "side-kick."

22. Fourth Street, the fourth card turned up.

23. Fifth Street, the last card turned up, also referred to as the River.

24. Razu, a colloquial term for raising the pot.

25. Cap, making the last of three raises before cards are turned after the flop and after each of the two last cards; also sometimes referred to as "cappuccino."

26. Button raise, refers to a player in the last position, marked by a white chip. The button rotates so that each player in turn is a "dealer."

27. Overkill, a hand that is way beyond what was necessary to win.

28. No-brainer, a hand which is patently easy to play and win.

29. One-jack-off, a hand that needs one more jack to make a winning hand but doesn't come up. It is intended to be a salacious pun but said so often that it has become a harmless cliché.

30. Cocka or kak-ka, a throw-away garbage hand.

31. Open-ended, referring to four sequential cards that need one more sequential card at either end of a hand to make a potential winner, and often said by a player to justify putting more chips in the pot and his losing, also called a "double-ender."

32. Double-gutter, nearly the same as the above except that either one of two related cards in the middle of a sequence is needed.

33. Big or Little Blind Specials, poor cards that win a pot for players who already had chips in before the betting and thus were automatically in the hand.

34. Outs, the number of possibilities for cards which could result in wins. It is usually said with respect to straights, flushes, and two pair.

35. The Nuts, a hand that cannot be beaten.

36. Drawing dead, refers to the best card a player can get and still lose.

37. Bad beat, vastly superior cards in a hand that is beaten by even better cards. Stories about these are endlessly recounted by players.

38. Tall Straight, the highest five sequential cards in a given hand.

39. Heads up, when only two players are contending.

40. All-in, signifying that a player bets, raises or calls with all his remaining chips.

41. String bet, when a player raises and in doing so places an insufficient amount of chips in the pot. His raise is canceled and he is forced to take back the extra chips.

42. Suited cards, two of the same suit.

43. Suited connections, two sequential cards of the same suit.

44. Runner-runner, the last two cards that are turned up which may enable the player to win.

45. Motown or Jackson Five, meaning a jack and a five.

46. Mop Squeezers or two queens, derived from the objects they appear to be holding in some decks of cards.

47. Highway Patrol or a ten and four.

48. Speed limit or two fives.

49. Sunset Strip or two sevens, after an old television series; also referred to as Walking Sticks.

50. Straddle or Live Blind, indicating that the person after the big blind raised before the cards were dealt and is entitled to raise again if he wishes before the flop of three common cards.

51. Pot odds, a calculation made by a player when the amount of chips in a pot is either very large are too little, which determines whether it is worthwhile to call or fold.

52. Checkens, or check, a variation of chickens.

53. Uptown, signifies a raise.

54. To fire out means a player has bet very quickly and aggressively.

55. Back door flush or straight, meaning a player has won because of the last three face-up cards.

56. Cheese, a poor hand.

57. A crying call, made by a player on the last betting and who expects to lose.

58. Donation, said by a player who calls but expects to lose.

59. Family pot, in which all players call the first bet.

60. Deadmeat, a hand that cannot win.

61. A "fisherman," someone who plays too many hands.

62. Colorado, means, "I call."

63. Pasadena, means, "I pass."

64. Big Lick, a six and nine as private down cards, an obvious sexual connotation.

65. Mid-life crisis or a pair of fours.

Special poker language and table talk mostly enlivens and not detracts from the game. These are constant and colorful features that appear to be intrinsic to gambling and poker. The mouths of most players are rarely closed; they are a very garrulous group. They of course need to use simple words like "pass," "check," or 'raise" which are the most common ones in poker. A common word seems to be "shit" which obviously indicates disgust and/or bad luck. I have selected phrases and sentences that I have heard while playing and that one hears repeated many times over. These constitute, as with the previous word list, a special kind of language and discourse in which the native speakers are all poker players and mostly privy to them only. They may be used by players to indicate frustration, praise, anger, sarcasm, impatience, and criticism. Their phrases may be insulting to or affirming of dealers and other players or they may be merely out loud mutterings. Unsolicited words of praise and/or commendations are constant in table talk. Some players deliberately use provocative language that stirs up passions and disrupts the game. Others are uttering words of "wisdom" or analysis of current events or comments on their personal life that most of us need not hear. And yet all of the above exist as poker becomes more and more popular. I expect the list presented below will grow. It is by no means an exhaustive list and is only confined to what I have experienced playing in the Oaks Club.

1. "Show one, show all," meaning once you expose your cards to anyone you should let everyone else at the table see them.

2. "One player to a hand," refers to those who are out of a hand but nevertheless comment on it.

3. "You play your cards and I'll play mine," usually said to a player who is commenting on how another plays.

4. "You're not in the pot," that is, "don't talk," about the hand in progress.

5. "I was rivered," meaning a player was defeated by the last card to be turned up, also known as "fifth street."

6. "Shit or get off the pot," demanding a player either act or throw his hand away. "Hold'em or fold'em" has the same meaning.

7. "Pump it or dump it," meaning either raise or "muck" your hand.

8. "Read'em and weep," a player with the winning hand sort of gloating over the losers.

9. "Send the cookies," said by a winner referring to the chips in the pot. Sometimes shortened to just "Send it!"

10. "I was ahead before the flop," an aimless lamentation from a losing player, meaning he initially had the best cards, but lost.

11. "I flopped it," meaning the player made a superior hand after the first three common cards. It can be the words of a winner or the disappointment of a loser.

12. "Give it up," a player urges others to throw their hands away because he thinks he has the best hand. Sometimes it is a phrase that may be said by someone who is bluffing.

13. "Check in the mail," said usually by the winner player after another player has checked. It is a kind of play on words.

14. "Who left that seat?" said by one or another player who have changed their seats while the new occupant wins. It is a joking phrase of self-incrimination; another way of phrasing it is, "Good seat change."

15. "Any two cards can win," a self-evident phrase that has become a cliché and is misleading for it is usually good cards that "win."

16. "Do you think if you hold onto your cards long enough their spots will change?", directed at a player who is slow to act.

17. "Play the rush," refers to a player who has just won and is an exhortation that if he continues to play will win several pots in succession.

18. "One time," an overused misleading phrase used by a player after calling, betting, or raising. It really means he will do so more than one time.

19. "Steam raise," a player who has just lost a hand and out of irritation wants to compensate for it quickly, usually an unwise move.

20. "He's on a tilt," said when a player aggressively and illogically plays out of frustration from losing.

21. "Meet me in the parking lot," said in jest when there is a minor altercation between two players. Another version is "Let's go outside." On rare occasions it is an actual threat.

22. "When are you leaving?" directed at a player who is winning or to a dealer by a player who is losing too much.

23. "She loved me," a phrase used by some females to the dealers who have dealt them a winning hand.

24. "Nice hand," a compliment said to a winner. However, sometimes the intent is sarcastic and quite opposite, particularly if it is seen as a clearly "poor" hand. Sometimes it sounds like "Nigh hand," which is a way of imitating how someone with a Chinese accent might pronounce it.

25. "Well, I was in the blind," an excuse by a player who wins a hand with poor cards.

26. "Do you think I would bet it for you?" said by the loser as a slight criticism of the winner who did not bet his winning hand, hoping to check and raise.

27. "I had too many outs," referring to a player's hand that had many ways of winning but does not.

28. "He never saw a hand he didn't like," criticism directed to a player that plays far too many hands.

29. "If you don't play the first hand you cannot win them all," another one of many ludicrous sentences uttered by poker players.

30. "Another winner!" said jokingly to a player who after losing far too many hands finally wins one.

31. "For one chip I would see a monkey flip over," said often by only one particular player to justify his putting one more chip in the pot and that is clearly a made-up rather nonsensical expression.

32. "I will keep you honest," said by a player to another when he calls a last bet with what is probably a losing hand.

33. "I am all over these cards," usually said by a player whose winning hand connected with many of the face-up cards.

34. "Don't touch my chips," said by a player when another player purposefully or accidentally touches his chips. This may be said in jest, but at times it is said angrily.

35. "I got trapped," said by a player who had a potentially winning hand to begin with but who is caught in the middle by others with better hands. It usually applies to a player who is pursuing a flush or a straight and fails to win. It is a kind of self-justification for putting so much money in the pot and still losing.

36. "Right off the street," said to a player who has just entered the game and won the first hand he played.

37. "Long time no eat," said by a player who has finally won a pot.

38. "I bought all these chips," said by a player in jest or seriously who has many, many chips and who has been asked where he got them all.

39. "That's a real hand," when a play compliments another player who often wins with mediocre cards but has now won with good cards such as a high pair.

40. "Nice river," said as criticism or praise to a player who wins the hand with the last open card.

41. "He jumped the fence," when a player does not play in turn.

42. "I had you beat," said by one player to another though they both lost the pot. In poker it is of no consequence who came in second.

43. "I was open-ended," said by a player who has four sequential cards in the hand and continues to play in the hope he will receive a fifth card at either end of his sequence to make him a winner. It is also said by a player whose hand is not completed.

44. "You have to be in it to win it," a cute sentence with an obvious meaning.

45. "I spiked it" or "I nailed it," meaning I suddenly got the card I wanted.

46. "You sucked out," said to a player who was behind all the way but who eventually won.

47. "I'm all in," meaning the player has put all his remaining chips into the pot, win or lose.

48. "There is no board," meaning a seat is available at a poker table but there are no players on the reservation list. Contrary to this is when a dealer raises his fist, his table is full, or he will indicate with his fingers how many seats are available.

49. "I have a monster," meaning a great hand.

50. "I bump it up," meaning to raise the pot.

51. "You were dead on arrival," meaning though you have a good hand on the flop someone has a better hand that you cannot possibly beat.

52. "You missed a bet," said somewhat sarcastically by a player implying that the winner should have bet more.

53. "It's not the seat, it's the player."

54. "I'll take it," said by a player who wins a small pot.

55. "Good lay-down," meaning a good hand that was thrown away because the player rightly thought it could not win.

56. "What did you have for breakfast, raisin bran?", refers to a player who does a great deal of raising.

57. "You get a lot of respect," said to a player who is not challenged or called by other players.

58. "I'll give you protection," said by one player who raises to another who is all-in and thus decreasing the competition.

59. "Does your husband play that well?", a criticism directed to a male player who wins with mediocre cards.

60. "Jack it up," means a raise.

61. "I'm in the dark," means a player bets or calls without looking at his cards.

62. "I'm a calling station," said by a player who calls many hands but doesn't win.

63. "I hate the game but love to play it."

64. "Unbelievable," a very overused word to describe the outcome of a hand.

65. "I've got my aces cracked," that is, they lost.

66. "Wave the lumber," referring to a player who has raised; a term used in baseball associated with the bat.

67. "I never leave home without one," said by a player who wins with a card usually an ace and is trying to be humorous.

68. "I'll test the waters," said by a player who raises or bets and by so doing hopes to determine what hands are out there. It is often a misleading statement.

69. "I had to call," said by a player as a thin excuse for calling or winning.

70. "I got lucky," a constantly overused phrase to indicate winning against the odds.

Some meanings are opposite of what they seem to be; rhetorical questions, cliches, excuses, justifications, and excessive table talk are all part of the game of poker. It is presented here as a special glossary of words, phrases, and sentences. The list could, I am sure, be lengthened, and I again welcome readers to do so. The spoken language and its verbal lore add an extremely colorful, human, and entertaining dimension to merely gambling and playing cards.

XIII. The Game Played: Texas Hold'em

Texas Hold'em has become the main poker game at the Oaks Club and many other casinos in California and elsewhere in the United States. In addition it has been described in many how-to-win books; there are some ten in print just devoted alone to this game. It is the featured game in most televised tournaments and online games provide many opportunities to learn about and play this poker game.

I have been unable to find the origins of Texas Hold'em. There is no reliable documentation that I have uncovered. The only explanation I have is anecdotal and was told to me by one regular player who came from Texas. It goes something like this. You start with the fact that a fifty-two card deck limits the number of players that can draw cards in games such as lowball, seven-card or five-card stud, Omaha, or five-card draw. Supposedly, cowboys on long and arduous cattle drives sought relief from boredom in the evenings and turned to poker. They devised a game that could accommodate more players, it was based on providing common five face-up cards that all players could use in addition to their two private ones. The object was to use the best five out of seven cards. Theoretically, you could have up to twenty-three players in the same poker game. This would be impractical for casinos which have limited space and where the established number has to be ten players. In the wide open dry spaces of Texas a poker game was supposedly born that has become the most popular one in the land. This then is only an untested tale of its origins. It seems as good as any explanation I have found so far but I need many more informants before I can vouch for it.

The popularity of Texas Hold'em may be based primarily on four elements. The first is the limited number of cards that can constitute a hand: two private and five common or open cards which any player can use. It is on the face of it a relatively simple game for determining whether you have promising cards with which to start and thus risk chips. Secondly, it is a dealer dealt game that provides more consistency and control for players. Thirdly, most regular players appear to agree that it is a simpler game that produces results more quickly compared to other games. It is may be an easier game to learn to play. However, above all it is an "action" game where betting can be fast and furious with ten players competing for success.

At the Oaks Club, there are nineteen tables devoted to poker, fourteen of them for Texas Hold'em. Bystanders are not allowed to hover near or watch up close any of the ongoing games. Most of the participants are regular players who daily play in various limit games such as 1/2, 2/4, 3/6, 6/12, and 15/30. Texas Hold'em has grown from its prohibition to the most popular poker game in the Oaks Club. Its popularity is increasing with media exposure in the so-called "World Series" tournaments. And it is reflected in the popularity of Texas Hold'em tournaments held throughout the year at the Oaks Club.

Tournaments have become a world of their own and the rewards and style of play are singularly different than regular poker games. Firstly, you need to start with much more money than ordinary because when you run out of chips you may need to buy more once or twice. If you lose them you are out. The stakes are much higher and the gambling is riskier. Ordinarily in Texas Hold'em tournaments there are usually no more than two or three players competing for a win in a hand in comparison with from five to ten participants in the games in which I regularly play. The competition is greater, the amount to be won is smaller, and the strategies of play less demanding than in tournaments. You can lose all your money in one hand in a tournament and be quickly eliminated. In contrast I can sometimes play five or six hours in the regular poker games without significant gains or losses. I am satisfied to play ordinary games with limited stakes and still dream, and dream only, of being a million dollar winner in some California or Nevada tournament. I have estimated roughly that there are in one year some 16,000 patrons of various limit Texas Hold'em games just in this one casino. It is by far my favorite poker game, win, lose, or break even. You might think of giving it a try. Be on notice that I am unavailable for instruction!

XIV. Bluffing and Cheating

Bluffing skillfully and randomly done is an important part of poker strategy. It involves betting amounts or raising in certain situations in which you cannot win unless you get your competition to throw their hands away. Bluffing works out best when you have only one or two opponents. If you do it excessively, you will be challenged and lose. Your ability to bluff successfully depends on a number of factors as follows:

1. selectivity, means judging the appropriate time to do it

2. the number of your opponents and their known styles of play

3. your seat position on any round of betting

4. the amount of chips you have compared to your competition

5. some intuitive sense influenced by past experiences as when to bluff or not.

The above is not intended as an instruction of how to bluff, rather it is a kind of description of what may take place. Bluffing represents a kind of acceptable player dishonesty that other players may begrudge and/or admire depending on outcomes. Obviously, a winning bluffing hand is by definition never shown. Only the player holding it knows the cards and he or she will rarely share them afterwards. The whole purpose of bluffing is to keep everyone in the dark about your style of play. It is probably an acquired skill coupled with a "poker face" and related emotional control. Bluffing is always problematic because there are so many factors governing its success. When I succeed at it there is an elation over "getting away with something" and in outsmarting others due to my cunning and timing. However, bluffers beware; there are always those who are better at it than you. You may become a victim rather than a winner.

Cheating is another matter for it is patently illegal in all casinos. Gambling, however, has cultivated within itself the possibility of beating the odds and bypassing conventional rules of play. Cheating at poker is an extremely difficult and risky undertaking. However, today in other forms of gambling such as roulette, dice, or pai gow it is practically impossible. Poker by its very nature requires some form of deception if players are to maximize their prospects for success. Cheating is a different matter but it could be viewed as an extension of poker tactics. It is difficult to cheat in a casino that has television cameras pointed at some tables and monitors that roam about as observers. The principal techniques of player cheating are marking the backs of cards and secretly using signals with another player such as facial expressions, hand gestures, or private code words. Usually such things are easy to detect, especially in a game where most of the regular players are well known to each other and to dealers and floor managers. Formerly, if at the end of play you called your hand as being higher than it actually was and caused the remaining player to throw his hand away, you could not win. It was considered a dishonest tactic if you did it on purpose. This rule has however been abolished. In any case you cannot win if you throw your cards away. It is now possible to use this "wrong call" as a tactic for winning. If you do this too often, the management will require that you do not do it again. There may be a kind of self-interest honor code at work among players which diminishes cheating because they themselves could be its victims. And, of course, management's reputation depends on a secure, safe, and well-protected game.

Some acts of cheating involve chips rather than cards. Players may secretly remove some of their chips from the table and pocket them to avoid losing too much in an ongoing hand. Then there are players who attempt to add chips to their stacks after they have seen their down cards or the flop to maximize the amount of money they can win in any pot. I have experienced both of these transgressions. These are relatively easy to spot because players can only buy chips before a hand is dealt and are forbidden to remove any of them unless they are leaving the game. Fortunately, the incidents of cheating are very uncommon at the Oaks Club and I have never seen any significant ones. I have been told that a dealer tried to cheat by manipulating cards so that jackpots were more likely to come. If successful he would benefit from the usual large tips given to him by the two involved players. His ruse was quickly discovered and, in any case, had been too difficult to hide. In addition, it is relatively unlikely that casino chips or cards can be counterfeited by anyone. General security in the card room and scrutiny of poker tables are the routine tasks of management. Poker playing was once a very devious activity with plenty of room for "card sharks" and cheaters. Today there is little evidence of this and in fact casinos may be one of the safest places in which to be and in which to routinely benefit from fair play and consistent card rules. The casino is not paradise but in dicey neighborhoods or hyped-up gambling centers one is reasonably safe. The only problem is the common possibility of losing money while feeling secure and comfortable at the same time in this environment.

XV. Chips, Charms, and Superstitions

The Oaks Club as do all other casinos require that only chips and not cash be used in gambling. Chips are uniformly sized but can be of various colors to distinguish those used in different limit games. The only size exception are the one hundred dollar chips which are bigger. All chips at the Oaks Club have an engraved metal center with the name of the casino and a simple design of an acorn. Chips can only be bought or added to one's stock before any hand is dealt. The dealer can sell chips for cash from his rack but most often a floor "chip person" supplies them to players or to the dealer. Players do all sorts of prohibited things with chips such as adding to or subtracting from them while they are playing a hand. Also a player cannot give or lend even one chip to another player. Players are permitted to pay waitresses with chips for service of food or drinks. If a player has acquired far too many chips from winning he may ask the "chip" person to exchange them for a higher denomination chip that takes up less room; this is called a "color change." However, within each game only one chip with the same value is used. Some players prefer to accumulate as many chips in front of them as possible. This may just be showing off their success or trying to intimidate other players. One's chips must be visible so that all the players and the dealer can if necessary determine the amount. I once chided a fellow player that he had too few chips with which to play. I said this mainly as a jest not a challenge. He was amused and his response was to buy many more chips than he needed. He playfully had turned the tables on me. Poker players are indeed "nefarious" persons.

The word chip has many nominal meanings, some derived from its medieval English origins as a piece of a wooden beam. These, however, seem to have little to do with how they became the coins of poker. The word is used in expressions such as "a chip off the old block," "chipping away" at some task, "chipping in" to indicate some contribution, and "to chip in," meaning to add something, a "chip on his shoulder," meaning someone who is irritable or haughty. This latter attribute is not uncommon in some poker players. I do not know how all of these definitions relate to the word "chip" in poker. Some of them do if you are willing to stretch your imagination. Please keep me informed.

A regular feature of Texas Hold'em games is the use of chips in what are called "blinds." Two players in turn must put out a fixed number of chips before any hand is dealt. In the 3/6 games the blinds are one and three dollars; in the 6/12 game they are four and six dollars. It rotates around the table so no one is disadvantaged. In addition, if you wish to play there is no way of avoiding your blind. If you leave the table and the blinds have passed beyond your seat, you must post their equivalent before you are dealt cards. Blinds help to insure that there is always some money in the pot before play commences. If no one bets before reaching the blinds the two last players remaining will usually "chop" them, that is to take back the chips and a new hand is dealt. It is a permitted convention but in tournaments or high stake games this is not allowed.

The limits in each Texas Hold'em game are fixed so that all possible bets can be made but under certain restrictions. For example, there can only be a maximum of three raises in any round of betting. This seems to supposedly diminish the power of players who have many chips from betting any more than is allowed. Raise and stake limits and rotating blinds enable more players to engage in a hand with less risk and to play more hands as well. The downside of limitations on raises is that the players starting with good or potentially winning hands cannot either diminish the number of competitors or protect them from hands which are far worse but may end up winning. In tournaments chips and higher limits generally preclude such outcomes. Limits work both ways to advantage and disadvantage all players. They also make it easier for patrons with limited resources to play poker. The Oaks Club, as do all casinos, has a major stake in seeing to it that there exists what is called a "level playing field" for all players. This means that all players have equal opportunities to win or lose chips under fair fixed rules.

Aside from representing money, another aspect of chips is just as interesting and seldom noticed. Chips can be regarded as the icons which represent a player's gain or losses at any given time. Betting and accumulating chips thus are certainly a constant measure of a player's progress but they can be used differently and can be seen in various other ways. Chips may be a psychological metaphor for a player's confidence, his self-esteem, or his fleeting grief, all of which are on public view. Players may place chips to protect their "hole" or down card from exposure or from mistakenly being mixed up with other hands. Players may bet chips to confuse play or intimidate their competitors. Some players, for example, handle chips before and while acting in a hand with a pause or movements to mislead what he or she is or is not intending to do. A player sometimes will "kiss his chips goodbye" as he throws them into the pot, signifying that they will probably never return to him. A chip antiseptic might be in order! A few players will buy more chips than required or play with very few. The former may be act of hubris while the latter may signify poverty or a strategy that enables to them to go "all in" more easily. Some players who are winning a great deal may keep as many chips as possible in front of them that is a kind of bragging or intimidation. Many players will throw or "splash" their bets in the center of a pot making it difficult for the dealer to determine if it was the proper amount. It may indicate a habit or an impatience or acting out on the part of a player. In any case, it delays the game and annoys dealers who have to sort out the chips. Often too few or too many chips are bet requiring corrections by the dealer, also slowing down the game. Players when betting may throw chips into the pot or slide them or roll them or methodically place them. There does not appear to be any significant reason for this variety; probably it is merely a habit. A few players will trade one chip with that of another player hoping it will bring them luck. Players are constantly rearranging and fondling their chips as if they were adored children or favorite pets. Children and chips need protection; pets and chips can be faithful companions. Most players understand the nominal value of chips and how to use them in betting. However, the use of chips involves a variety of often curious behaviors, beliefs, and practices. Most of them appear to have little to do with the actual playing of poker and the examples are many and intriguing.

When players enter a game, they buy chips and arrange them in various stacks in front of them. The usual arrangements are mostly vertical either without any intended order or in uniform stacks of ten or twenty. However, chip arrangements can be extremely diverse. I have seen chips arranged as columns, pyramids, triangles, rectangles, octagons, hexagons, cloverleafs, and other geometric forms. Some may resemble, among others, twin towers, high-rise office buildings, monuments, steps, or walls. It is as if among players there are amateur engineers, frustrated architects, part-time mathematicians, and stone worshippers. One player carefully placed a blue chip on top of each of his gray chip stacks. When asked why, he said, "To protect them." Another player placed a rubber band around twelve chips in a 6/12 game. He called this a "bomb" and when rolled into the pot as a raise, it indicated a "monster" hand. Some players are quite creative, even obsessive, about their mini-constructions. I saw one player who always arranged his chips in the form of an octagon that he kept at least six inches high in front of him. When he would lose chips he replaced them immediately to retain the "integrity" of his beloved octagon. When I asked why he did this, he said, "Eight is my lucky number." Another player in his blind placed his three chips upright with two delicately supporting the other. It stayed balanced this way until his blind went into the pot. When I asked him about it, he said, "It brings me luck and makes me feel good." Many arrange chips in vertical stacks of ten, twenty, and forty and also horizontally extend them in little piles.

Another variation is lining up stacks so they extend outwardly like a long fishing pier. Some players methodically stack their chips so that the design on their edges show uniformly and keep them this way all the time. One of the strangest arrangements I have seen involved a player who had won many chips piling them in vertical stacks of one hundred and twenty or more. He built them up so high that they literally rested just under his chin. To keep them upright is no small feat in California earthquake country. At one point this same player actually dozed off for a few moments resting his chin precariously on his chips. Two of the more creative and elegant chip arrangements I have seen formed some fantastic structures. One was like a ten-inch high totem pole with single chips extended out like rounded arms in all directions. The second was an elaborate structure resembling a temple entrance or portal about one foot high and six inches wide. Over the entrance was a kind of lintel on top of which were balanced chips and at the sides were others extending outwards. It reminded me of the impressive entrances to Hindu temples in India and Bali. If nothing else it was an extraordinary balancing feat. When asked what these structures meant or why he did them, he answered somewhat tongue-in-cheek, "I get bored." Perhaps the most attractive one I have seen was that of two eight-inch-high stacks of chips, each arranged like a perfect spiral staircase. This was a particularly remarkable feat in that the player in question had been playing for more than thirteen hours. I have no ready explanation for all these chip arrangements. It may be they fulfill fantasies, are habits reflected in superstitions, are representative of careers not pursued, or are merely individual idiosyncrasies. Psychologists might be tempted to characterize and explain their meanings. After all, there are ink-blots that are used to decode human behavior so why not apply them to chip arrangements in poker. This may see a bit facetious on my part, but I have been particularly intrigued with what players do with their chips. I will not offer any conclusions because yet I haven't formed any. I might devise an adult game called "Chips and Persons." Let me know if you invent a similar one.

Players are always attempting to improve their poker prospects by means other than good cards and smart play. One way they do this is to use good luck charms or talismans. They may be used to protect themselves and their hole cards or just try to affect good outcomes. Casino rules do not allow foreign objects on the table but this is rarely enforced if the items are small and unobtrusive. Only a few players, usually no more than one or two at a table, use them. Some players appear to be ardently devoted to their charms or talismans, some of which they change from time to time. Their efficacy is, however, problematic unless you are a true believer or merely enjoy these as harmless gimmicks.

These charms and objects constitute a veritable Pandora's box of little people, tiny animals, metal objects, astrological symbols, and other small and odd pieces. They clearly are not used merely to prevent exposure of hole or down cards. Below is a partial list of those that I have seen at the Oaks Club while playing Texas Hold'em. They include the following: a rabbit's foot, a chip with a royal flush imprinted on both sides, a plastic green cloverleaf, a plastic figure of Colossus, a replica of an old-fashioned metal golf tee, a silver wedding ring, a rubber nun, a Chinese porcelain dog, a chip with a joker figure on one side, a slot machine coin, two clear glass Chinese Buddhas (one pink, the other green), a plastic Japanese god of happiness, a chip with the date 1995 marking the 100th anniversary of the Oaks Club, a round jade symbol, a Hawaii hotel token, a colored plastic bearded old man, an Indonesian medallion, a bus token, silver U.S. and Mexican coins, a brown glass horse on a Chinese stand, a brass whistle, a German five-mark piece, a Mah Jong tile, a cigarette, a lighter, a toy airplane, an aluminum angel, an ace of diamonds that can be spun inside a chip with a metal frame, a rubber lizard and spider, a doll with a moveable head, an NRA medallion, a miniature No.13 pool ball cut in half, a Japanese ivory *netsuke* of a mother monkey and her baby, an enameled joss stick holder from India, a silver medallion commemorating in Hebrew the 6-day war on one side and the Wailing Wall on the other, a beer bottle cap, chips or tokens from another casino, car keys, cell phones, a miniature silver King Arthur, a small box of live ladybugs, a JFK half dollar, a chip imprinted with the columns of the Egyptian Luxor temple, a Mars Space Rover medallion, a quartz crystal, a one-pound enlarged sterling medallion with the date April 1912 showing the sinking of the Titanic on one side and an ace of diamonds engraved on the other, a chip commemorating a family reunion in Oklahoma with a grandfather and grandmother on one side and "Bar S Ranch" on the other, a rubber squeeze ball for stress, an hour glass, a university graduation medal and, finally, a plastic object replete with flags and patriotic words commemorating the catastrophe of September 11. Scour the casinos and no doubt many more will turn up.

Most charms are not at all even vaguely functional but reflect the multiple, sometimes superstitious or humorous attempts of players to increase their success or liven up their play. In doing this they may use almost anything that helps besides skill and chance. I have used a talisman (e.g., a tiny bottle of nitroglycerin pills) on occasion but it did not seem to bring me any benefits. When I asked questions about charms I received answers such as, "My son gave it to me for good luck," "My grandfather used it before me," "It keeps me company," "It has brought me luck in the past," and lastly that profound answer, "Why not?" Clearly poker is wrapped up in superstition. The lack of skills, the burdens of bad luck, the shortage of money, and the arbitrariness of chance are all part of the deep longings of gamblers to improve their play and reap great rewards. Talismans, "lucky" seats, seat changes, "lucky" dealers, favorite cards, selecting the best playing times on particular days, praying, and bluffing are all in the name of using any resources and methods to succeed. One seemingly nervous player had two pieces of chert which he smoothed out with sandpaper from time to time. Perhaps the most endearing good luck charm I have encountered was a metal object in the shape of a chip on which was engraved "I love you," "Biscuit," and "Sweet Pea." It was given to a male player (Biscuit) by his loving wife (Sweet Pea). Another one in the same mode was a 1978 gold-plated silver dollar commemorating the marriage date of the player and his wife. What an entertaining and marvelous bunch we poker players are!

To close this chapter I will describe the strangest and most humorous charm that I have encountered. It was a cockroach that had been embedded on purpose in an oblong piece of clear, polished plastic. The owner of this object indicated it came about when he retrieved it from a bowl of minestrone soup that he had been served. He had it preserved forever, a kind of memento that would never have occurred to me but is vastly entertaining. Go out and find the appropriate bug or buy mysterious objects from the secret world. Please let me know if they work; I will buy and pay the postage for any.

XVI. Epilogue

As long as there are ordinary people with fanciful dreams in the search of great rewards and exciting adventures there will always be gamblers and poker players. Gambling in its various forms probably ranks just behind sex and sports as the primary preoccupation of males in American society. Playing cards for money has escaped from its former status as a wrongful or sinful activity. It has emerged instead as an exciting, intriguing, and proper form of recreation and entertainment for many ages and groups. The United States appears to have the highest per capita number of poker players in the world. Gambling casinos are springing up everywhere and continuing this expansion seems inevitable. Obtaining the perfect hand, winning an enormous pot, and outwitting all competitors are writ large in the minds of many men and an increasing number of women. People play in private homes, on boats and trains, card clubs, casinos, and on the Internet. The U.S. is fast becoming a poker nation.

I have shared with you the many steps along my poker trail. Now in my late years I continue to play poker every Wednesday with friends in a backyard garage and several times a week in a large casino, the Oaks Club. These two places are probably my last hurrahs for playing poker. Both have provided me with a kind of peace of mind, considerable comradeship, a temporary relief from the ailments of aging, and have not drained my bank account. There has been both disappointment and joy in my experiencing poker. I make no great claims for it, for my salvation or for anybody else's. My family has tolerated my gambling with both disapproval and equanimity. I hope all of you out there can be so lucky!

In diverse attire anonymous Poker men,

sit around a green-covered table,

all fellow travelers pilgrimaging in and

out of small dim-lit places and

grandiose rooms.

A journey never ending

until all the cards are gone

and all the games are over.

978-0-595-39123-3
0-595-39123-0

Printed in the United States
69138LVS00004BA/321

9 780595 391233